Management for Professionals

More information about this series at http://www.springer.com/series/10101

Vanessa Ratten

Sport Entrepreneurship

Developing and Sustaining an Entrepreneurial Sports Culture

 Springer

Vanessa Ratten
Department of Entrepreneurship,
Innovation and Marketing
La Trobe University
Melbourne, Victoria
Australia

ISSN 2192-8096   ISSN 2192-810X   (electronic)
Management for Professionals
ISBN 978-3-319-89227-6   ISBN 978-3-319-73010-3   (eBook)
https://doi.org/10.1007/978-3-319-73010-3

This Springer imprint is published by Springer Nature
The registered company is Springer International Publishing AG
The registered company address is: Gewerbestrasse 11, 6330 Cham, Switzerland

Endorsements

Sports is not only an area of interest worldwide, but is one of the largest revenue producing industries globally. The field of entrepreneurship has moved beyond business startup to being an integral part of both small and large businesses. Dr. Ratten's book, Sport Entrepreneurship, explores the role of entrepreneurship in sport by focusing on how new products emerge in the market and the role of innovation. The book not only helps to understand why the sport's industry has so many new products and services, but the multiple of ways that it influences our lives and other industries. Key topics such as business model innovation are discussed in terms of the sport environment. The book is a must-read for anyone in sports or business.

Dr. Arthur Rubens
Professor Emeritus, Fulbright Scholar (Slovakia), Florida Gulf
Coast University, Lutgert College of Business, Fort Myers, Florida

Dr. Vanessa Ratten's book is a must-read for businesses and researchers interested in sport entrepreneurship. She emphasizes the changing landscape of sport and encourages researchers to examine how entrepreneurship can influence the overall operation and success of the sport industry. She also calls on researchers to utilize other disciplines to develop and expand the field of sport entrepreneurship. Anyone who is interested in sport entrepreneurship will value this book, as it provides a unique glimpse into how entrepreneurship is intertwined with sport business and research.

Natasha T. Brison, JD, PhD, Texas A&M University

Foreword

First a disclaimer. In my self-deprecating moments, I sometimes refer to myself as "the least entrepreneurial person on the planet". However, there is no limit to my admiration of entrepreneurs. I am drawn to their passion, drive, resilience, creativity and self-reliance. My first entrepreneurial hero was Dan Empfield, inventor of the triathlon-specific wetsuit in 1987 and the triathlon-specific racing bike in 1989. Not only did he have the technical and engineering skills to invent these products, he also had the business skills to make more than a little bit of money from his inventions.

Twenty-five years ago an undergraduate student told me she wanted to be an entrepreneur, but she did not know how to be one. Twenty-five years ago I said "I think that is a big part of being an entrepreneur...you have to figure many things out for yourself, there is no blueprint". If I was asked that question today, I would probably say the same things, but add "You might want to read this book".

This is a perfect time for a book about sport entrepreneurship to hit the shelves. Entrepreneurship is a major force of the global economy. The global sports industry continues to expand, challenged by the notion of being both bigger and better. The sports industry is many things—inspiring, engaging and emotional. There is no business like the sports business, and this book will provide readers with a head start, an informed start on creating value, either to make money or to improve the world.

The global sports industry renews itself constantly. This book will inspire conversations, not just between researchers but also between and amongst researchers, policymakers, managers and entrepreneurs.

This is the first book on sport entrepreneurship. But it is certainly not the first academic writing on the subject. The irony of this is that most of the academic writing on sport entrepreneurship already belongs to Vanessa Ratten. She is synonymous with sport entrepreneurship, having authored over 100 articles and book chapters related to entrepreneurship. This makes her not just an authority on the topic of sport entrepreneurship, this makes her the authority.

Entrepreneurship is not just a theoretical concept. It is a living, a lifestyle, a mindset and key, not just to a better sports industry but also to a better world. To this end, we are fortunate to have both Vanessa and this book.

Auckland University of Technology   Geoff Dickson
Auckland, New Zealand

Acknowledgements

The writing of this book has been a long journey started many years ago but only recently coming to fruition. I thank my mum Kaye Ratten for enabling me to be educated and for encouraging me to follow my dreams. I am very grateful for her and recognize the value of education but also acknowledge her help and support. I also thank my dad David Ratten for finding news items related to sport entrepreneurship, which have been helpful examples used in this book. I am grateful to my brothers Hamish Ratten and Stuart Ratten for telling me what I should and should not be doing as younger brothers do to their older sister. Finally, I thank my colleagues and friends who have encouraged me to write this book. Thank you.

Contents

An Introduction to Sports Entrepreneurship 1

1.1 Introduction

Entrepreneurship has received increased interest from sports managers and researchers, indicating the important role that entrepreneurship plays within the sports industry for value creation. Despite the practical significance of entrepreneurship to sports, the literature on sports entrepreneurship remains fragmented and underdeveloped. There has only recently been an interest by sports management researchers to integrate entrepreneurship literature within their discipline. However, the interest in sports entrepreneurship is growing quickly with different perspectives from the social, international and technological dimensions being integrated into the literature. Sports entrepreneurship is different to other types of entrepreneurship due to the emotional nature of sport and has both a profit and non-profit role in society (Miragaia et al. 2017). Thus, specific theoretical and managerial insights from a distinct sports entrepreneurship approach are needed.

Sport entrepreneurship involves a transition from current practices to more of an innovative behavioural model (Ratten 2010). Innovation involves change but in the sports context it can vary from developing new teams, introducing ideas or changing work practices. The reason for increased interest in entrepreneurship in sport is due to the sport industry being one of the largest and most changing because of its competitive nature (Ratten 2011). There are continually new technology and consumer demands in sport that impacts on the development of new ideas to serve growing markets. The traditional sport products include clothing and equipment, which have been influenced by the adoption of more technological and user-oriented innovations. In addition, there is an increasing demand for innovative sport-based products and services that utilize emerging technology. This has led to there being increased curiosity by governments and local regional authorities about creating a sports entrepreneurial ecosystem that enables new venture creation.

Sports entrepreneurship as a field of study has been slowly emerging but has recently blossomed as there is recognition of sport as having an entrepreneurial spirit (Ratten 2012). In order to advance research and practice on sports entrepreneurship a

© Springer International Publishing AG 2018
V. Ratten, *Sport Entrepreneurship*, Management for Professionals,
https://doi.org/10.1007/978-3-319-73010-3_1

more systematic understanding about its features is needed. The objective of this chapter is to provide an overview of entrepreneurship in the sport industry, analyzing the current trends and suggestions to move the discipline forward. The literature about entrepreneurship in the context of sport is discussed that shows the changing nature of sports entrepreneurship research. The chapters of this book are then summarized and directions for future sports entrepreneurship research stated.

1.2   The Development of Sport

A general definition of sport refers to using physical activity as "a large segment of the body, or the entire body, is coordinated and integral to the successful completion of the task" (Jenny et al. 2016: 10). This emphasis on the physical aspects is inherent in most definitions of sport. In addition, sport can exist on a continuum from low to high impact based on the degree of physicality. Low impact sports are those will little physical activity and are slower in nature. For example, walking or bowling, which can be done with little energy. In contrast, high impact sports include those with a lot of physical exertion that require people normally to train in order to perform the sport. There is some debate though about how to define a sport due to the stereotypes over high impact sport being more physical whilst low impact sports can be sometimes categorized as more recreational. This is emphasized by Hemphill (2005: 196) who stated that real sports are "sport that involves the most face-to-face aggression, power and body contact".

Sports can be casual or organized forms of participation. Increasingly more people want to experience sport in a casual form without any kind of commitment. This is due to people working different hours to the past and this unpredictability affects their ability to play sport. There are casual gym memberships that have grown in popularity and this has influenced the emergence of casual classes or other types of sport. In the past many sports were a set number of weeks or times of the day but this has changed as more people want the flexibility to play sport at alternative times of the day (Ratten 2017a). This is seen in some sports that were previously weekly events like netball having casual time slots. Hence, more people can attend the game but at the same time it creates the risk that it will be a one off event.

Sport can be played indoors or outdoors depending on the situation and climate. Indoor sports are typically more popular in colder climates as it is harder to play outdoors. However, some sports are specifically designed to be played indoors such as indoor soccer or trampoline. Outdoor sports use the natural environment as part of the playing experience. This means that wind and sun have an effect on the ability of athletes to perform outdoors. Some sports such as aerobics that were typically conducted indoors have moved to outdoors as a form of new experience. This has resulted in increased interest in the sport of aerobics as it is conducted in a different environment. The outdoors environment is a new atmospheric that enables the use of land for sport, which is often free rather than the indoors sports facilities that people typically have to pay for.

Sports are characterized by having some form of play and normally rules that regulate behavior (Ratten and Babiak 2010). With the increased usage of technology in sport this adds an additional dimension about how to define sport. Research by Jenny et al. (2016: 5) states that play includes "voluntary, intrinsically motivated activity which is performed for fun or enjoyment". Most people perceive sport as being a form of entertainment and they can play or watch the games. Sometimes there is an interchange between the word sport and game depending on the situation and context. However, normally all forms of sport are considered a game but might differ in length and style of play. Jenny et al. (2016) suggests that there are some defining characteristics of sport including play, organization, competition, skill, having a following and achieving institutional stability. The play can occur in a physical or online environment depending on the type of sport. Some sports have longer play periods such as cricket that can occur over a couple of days. Other sports have shorter time periods and this is reflected in the nature of the sport. Play can be voluntary or mandated depending on the sport context. Some informal sports such as skateboarding, which has moved into a formal competition like structure is played differently compared to sports like tennis that have set structures. This means that there will be different motivations to play sport depending on the weather conditions and type of competition (Ratten and Ratten 2011). In some sport competitions there is continual play periods whilst others occur over a longer time period and rely on the performance of the sports players.

Sport is structured by rules that are the same and only change by consensus when the timing is right. This means that the rules ensure a fair playing system and means that spectators can understand the play as it occurs. The rules of sport are changing because of different tastes and preferences influencing the game. This is reflected in replay technology being used in football to evaluate if a ball actually goes over the goal line. In tennis decisions of the referees can be challenged using technology to see if the decision was correct. Sport is a form of competition that normally has a winner and loser. This competitive spirit is part of the reason why sport is enjoyed around the world. The unknown element of who will win a competition has created other industries including online gaming and fantasy sports. Some informal sports are less competitive with the emphasis on play rather than the end result. This means in some solitary sports such as surfing the competition is rather with oneself than with a team or group of people although they may be playing at the same time. There are formal surfing competitions but this differs to the informal way it is often conducted.

Sport needs to include a skill that is increased when played over a time period. Some people have natural skills and are more suited to certain types of sport. The skills needed to play sport differ from hitting a ball to swimming or climbing a cliff. These skills occur not by chance but rather as a result of deliberate action. In addition, there is a degree of subjectivity about what skills are harder to master in a sports context and this often depends on the financial capacity of a sport. Sports such as football only need a ball but are often played in high cost arenas to ensure higher spectator rates at the games. Other sports such as skiing might require more equipment and be expensive to play.

There is a form of physical activity in the skills needed to play some sports. Sports such as running require a lot of energy whilst croquet is less physically intensive. The physical aspect of sport has given rise to other industries related to the game such as sports drinks or nutrition bars designed to give athletes more energy during games. The physical aspect of sport means that there is attention placed on an athlete's body and sometimes injuries can destroy their career. For this reason some sports such as baseball use pitchers for a short time period in order to lengthen their playing career. There are pitchers in baseball called closers that are also brought into games at the end in order to achieve high impact performance pitches.

Sport needs to have a group of people who follow it in order for it to be considered a sport. This means that sports grow based on their popularity amongst their followers. Moreover, sport has internationalized as people move to new geographic areas and bring their love of a sport to an area. This is seen with ice hockey teams moving to warmer climates in the United States especially in the south of the country because there have been a large number of people living there who moved from colder climates but still want to watch the sport. Thus, some cities or regions have invested in sports facilities as a way of drawing more people into their region. This is reflected with sports tourism become a growing industry. Some locations such as Nazare in Portugal have seen how followers of surfing can transform an area into an internationally recognized sports destination. The followers of a sport differ in terms of demographics and are increasingly located globally due to the ease of watching sport on television. Sports such as football have followers based on family connections and the reasons for following a certain sport team are passed down generations. Lifestyle sports such as yoga have a following that is tied into the idea of spirituality in sport. This means that yoga has less rules than other sports and this is the reason for its followers liking the sport.

1.3   Sport as a Formal and Informal Activity

Sport has both a formal and informal nature, which influences entrepreneurial endeavours. At the formal level there are well established sport organizations that function based on rules and procedures. Informal components of sport involve the more ad-hoc industries that develop depending on cultural conditions. There is also a tendency to characterize sport based on physical activity but there has been a trend towards more electronic forms due to technological innovations. Thus, sport is valued by society as it is reflected in fan engagement, usage of facilities and consumer spending power. Internationally sport is defined by its experiential and intangible experience that makes it unique. Thus, there is a subjective element to sport due to the many different types. This means sport can be both consumed and produced depending on the context. The consumption of sport involves playing it in a physical or electronic form.

Traditionally sport was considered as a physical activity and people needed to play in a face-to-face environment. This has changed with the internet and communications technology as people play games in an electronic environment. The production of sport means being involved in a game either as a player or regulator. Much of this production occurs in a social environment that is based on the exchanged forms of play. In addition, there is an unpredictability of sport and this is part of its appeal. The inconsistency in the way sport is played and consumed varies based on the international context. Some cultures value certain types of sport more than others and this is reflected in the businesses that develop. For example, football is considered one of the most popular forms of sport globally but the way it is played varies by country. This means football in Europe differs to the type played in the United States. Other sports might be more based on weather conditions and be suited to certain types of climate. In Australia and Brazil surfing is popular due to the beach culture and climate. In Norway and colder climates skiing is more popular.

Sport provides social and normally physical types of activity. Depending on the resources sport can be played in a variety of geographical settings and is either formal or informal in nature. When sport is played there normally needs to be an exchange between the conduct and rules of the game, which is governed by the players or external referees. Often sport is authoritarian and bureaucratic with set rules that need to be obeyed. Increasingly people are using sport in an entrepreneurial way to provide more opportunities and generate additional revenue. Thus, there have been traditionally established practices of sport that are changing as a result of challenges. This includes the increasing numbers of people who like to see innovation in sport as a form of entertainment.

The new entrepreneurial trends in sport have changed the nature of sport. The alterations in sport have been influenced by better accessibility via the internet and technology. Thus, there are value and positive implications associated with entrepreneurship in sport. This is due to there being an increasing convergence of business, culture and technology in sport (Jenny et al. 2016). Moreover, sport is considered as both a physical activity but also an online or media based game. eSports are classified as "electronic sports, cybersports, gaming, competitive computer gaming and virtual sport" (Jenny et al. 2016: 1). In sport there are new technological options changing the way games are played and managed. This is reflected in new electronic and physical infrastructures being developed to manage the technological innovations. As there is an abundance of new information coming into the marketplace, technology is a way of filtering this knowledge in order to choose the most appropriate innovative ideas.

1.4   The Role of Entrepreneurship in Sport

There are three main views of entrepreneurship: innovation-based, business formation and opportunity recognition (Solvoll et al. 2015). The innovation-based view focuses on the role of change and newness as part of entrepreneurship. This was originally developed by Schumpeter (1934) who wrote about the role of entrepreneurs as innovators. Sometimes the innovation-based view is referred to as Schumpeterian economics due to the emphasis on reconfiguration of resources for change. The main thread in the innovation-based view is that entrepreneurs create change through innovation that enables differentiation in the marketplace. Innovations are a key part of sport due to new sports being developed that transform existing practices. In addition, due to the role winning and competition plays in sport, innovation provides a way for individuals and organizations in sport to remain competitive.

The second view is the business formation perspective, which views entrepreneurship as essentially being focused on business creation. The creation of new businesses is a way entrepreneurship is distinguished from innovation. In sport, there are new businesses being developed based on new ideas but also changes in technology and societal expectations. This means that business formation is crucial to the sports industry that needs to establish new ventures that influence profitability. Sometimes the new sport businesses might be adopted from existing ones or they might involve the creation of separate entities.

The third view is the opportunity-based perspective, which focuses on the discovery process. The acknowledgement then commercialization of business opportunities is important for sport. Often some ideas about sport might take time to be exploited or alternatively they are time sensitive and need to be exploited quickly. The finding of good opportunities about sport that bring revenue and prestige are important to an entrepreneur's reputation. This means the opportunity-based view of entrepreneurship takes a broad perspective about what is possible in sport.

Entrepreneurship is a broad business related topic that takes a variety of forms including community, institutional, social, sustainable and technological. Only recently has sport entrepreneurship been considered as another sub-topic of entrepreneurship studies. Sport can be considered as a phenomenon or passion rather than purely as an industry. This is due to the disparate nature of sport as a product and service depending on the context. Therefore, specific theories need to be developed for sport entrepreneurship due to its contextual and unique elements. The link between sport and entrepreneurship is seldom made although it is growing in significance due to recent studies on the topic (Ratten 2017b). Only recently has there been a use of the sport-based theory of entrepreneurship in mainstream sports journals.

The sport industry has specific characteristics including the need for a high level of government support to build stadiums and related venues. This means that there can be a time lag between the recognition of sports entrepreneurship and its development in the marketplace. In addition, many sports are played on a seasonal basis so this affects the ability of sport entrepreneurs to seize opportunities. This has led to there being an increased usage of multi-media communications technology in sport and this is often linked to a need for a high level of investment.

Sport entrepreneurship has a practical approach due to its anchoring in business management. The research on sports entrepreneurship can be advanced by building on existing entrepreneurship theories that can be integrated into a sports context. Thus, the sports entrepreneurship field can benefit from the development of more practical and theoretical usage. In sport, there is often a dependence on the location to experience or play sport, which affects the creation of new businesses.

There is an entrepreneurial characteristic of the sports industry from incorporating gender, racial and equality policies to the development of new clothing. Some of the most famous sports entrepreneurs include Phil Knight from Nike who created a sportswear company and the iconic swoosh logo to Michael Jordan who created his own shoe that is still a best seller despite him no longer playing professional sport. There are also well known sports franchises such as NASCAR in car racing that pioneered the use of innovation materials in tyres and cars to newer sports such as the Ultimate Fight Championship that televises mixed martial arts events often paid-per-view, which is one of the fastest growing sports in the world. These sport entrepreneurs and enterprises have made sport synonymous with change and innovation.

Most of the existing entrepreneurship and innovation literature has focused on the manufacturing industry and less on service businesses (Hjalager 2010). This is despite sport becoming more of a service industry due to the increased usage of information technology. The use of emerging technologies and entrepreneurship has gained in popularity for being buzz words used by organizations and governments to convey change. The sports industry has been later in utilizing entrepreneurship concepts from other fields. More sport policy and practice has recognized the valuable contribution of entrepreneurs and this is transferring to the academic literature.

Entrepreneurship research provides a way of understanding the innovations within sport and helps to bring more attention to the benefits of change. There is a lack of consensus about what innovation is due to its wide usage and varying meanings. Most definitions of innovation focus on the process of solving a problem or bringing about change through creative ideas. In order for innovation to occur it needs to be generated then accepted by an entity that has the capacity to change (Hjalager 2010). This means that the discontinuance of previous practices by favouring new ways of thinking is at the center of innovation studies (Johannesson et al. 2001). Most studies about entrepreneurship in sport still rely on traditional views of entrepreneurship rather than tailoring it to the sports context. For example, Hjalager (2010: 2) states "adding a summer season to winter sports destinations may be considered a far-reaching innovation". There is an incomplete understanding of the entrepreneurial process in sport including how it differs to other industries.

There is often more consumer and business interaction in sport than other sectors, which influences the entrepreneurship process. Sport managers need to be more aware about entrepreneurial strategies that they can utilize to increase overall performance. Technology represents a key factor influencing entrepreneurship but affects sport in different ways. Sport entrepreneurship research needs to incorporate emerging technology through a more interdisciplinary approach due to the investigation of entrepreneurship being not strongly represented in existing sports research.

Entrepreneurship research in sport is a young phenomenon with little collective knowledge developed by scholars. There are issues about sports entrepreneurship that are evident in practice but less understood by researchers. To promote entrepreneurship in sport there is a need for businesses to encourage creative thinking. Consumers particularly those in sport who tend to have a higher level of loyalty than other sectors can collaborate with sports teams to come up with new ideas.

1.5   Sport and Process Innovations

Hjalager (2010: 2) states "process innovations refer typically to backstage initiatives which aim at escalating efficiency, production and flow". In sport, process innovations especially in terms of service delivery have transformed the industry but enabled the use of more communications technology. This has influenced sport to broaden its international appeal as information can transcend geographic and time boundaries. More efficient technology systems are useful to sport organizations when partnered with existing strategies. Sports organizations often declare themselves as entrepreneurial as a way to strengthen their brand and service offerings. It also helps them by refocusing attention onto their organization by stressing new products or services.

Sport innovations often involve the combination of sport and destination marketing through entrepreneurship. Entrepreneurship plays an important role in the evolution of sports products and services. Some sports such as surfing have developed because of their entrepreneurial process nature.

Entrepreneurship is considered by stakeholders in a sports context as a way to stimulate growth by encouraging collaboration. Entrepreneurship can be analyzed "in the micro (individual), meso (industry or region) or macro (country or group of countries) level" (Dvoultey 2017: 12). At the micro level sports entrepreneurship focuses on how individuals develop new ventures about sport. The meso level means that some regions are focusing specifically on sports entrepreneurship whilst the macro level requires a group of countries collaborating on an innovation in sport.

Some entrepreneurs in sport start with few resources and use innovation as a way to grow their business. However, there is corporate entrepreneurship in sport that enables larger organizations to use their existing resources for new business ventures. Some sports have been more entrepreneurial due to the leadership of managers that have encouraged a try, fail and try again approach. Some sport entrepreneurs utilize their own experience to introduce innovations in the industry. In sport, normally market demand determines the type and level of entrepreneurship. Increasingly customization is an important part of sports entrepreneurship. This is due to the personalization of technology devices used by consumers in a sport context. Sometimes sport fans innovate and become the first movers, which is then adopted by other audiences. After a sports innovation has been introduced into the market it can be changed depending on consumer preferences. This enables consumers to try and explore the sports innovation.

The long term growth of the sports industry requires participation from entrepreneurs in order to ensure prosperity. Entrepreneurship is a way organizations and governments can influence sport because new businesses play a crucial role in increasing the competitiveness of the sports industry. There is a great need for new ideas about sports entrepreneurship as a promising area of research. Sport develops and transforms communities especially when it is entrepreneurial. Sport entrepreneurship creates ways to change economic and social conditions to bring about positive change. Thus, sport entrepreneurship offers a way to solve market challenges that require new thinking.

Both sports practitioners and researchers are emphasizing the growing importance of entrepreneurship. The sports entrepreneurship research area has undergone major advances with more studies focusing on the need for an entrepreneurial perspective in sport. However, there are still many crucial areas of research about sports entrepreneurship that have received little attention. Thus, it is important to integrate the concepts of creativity and innovation in sport to advance research in these areas. Rank et al. (2004: 519) defines creativity as "the production of new and useful ideas by an individual or small group of individuals working together". Creativity is the step before innovation as it involves generating ideas and the introduction of novel thoughts. Often creativity focuses on intra-individual cognitive processes but innovation is about inter-individual processes. This means that there tends to be more social interaction in innovation due to the intentional application of new ideas.

In a sport context, the innovation is designed to benefit individuals, groups or organizations depending on the environment. To utilize both creativity and innovation in the marketplace there needs to be a translation of actions and intentions into goals (Rank et al. 2004). The moods and emotional state of an individual or organization can affect the development of creativity. This is due to positive moods having a contagion effect to spur creativity but negative moods making creativity a necessity for survival. Thus, depending on the sports context, positive moods may encourage further creativity from advances and influence more energy towards innovation (Rank et al. 2004).

Some demands such as urgency and competition affect creativity in both a positive and negative manner depending on the situation. For example, sport organizations that compete with each other or are interested in finding a mutually beneficial solution to a problem are likely to be more creative. In addition, some sport leaders may be more influential in encouraging creativity as people are comfortable speaking up without fear or retaliation. This means that sport leaders are important in influencing the level and type of creativity that is needed for entrepreneurship. Some sport leaders especially coaches are known to be visionaries and utilize creativity in a positive way. This helps with idea generation but also enabling others to discuss potential solutions.

There are several stages in the innovation process that require creativity including the promotion of strategies, finding funding and developing schedules for implementation. In sport, often athletes and coaches come up with creative ideas but they need institutional or financial support for it to progress. Thus, sports clubs often partner with organizations that can offer the business advice needed for the innovation. Creativity is comprised of task identification, preparation, response generation, response validation and communication. In sports, some task styles of play or equipment may be creative at first but then gain quick acceptance by users because of their affect on performance. This is seen in baseball catchers wearing nail polish on their hands so the pitcher can see signals more easily. Whilst creative it is a practical solution in a sport that utilizes signals for the game. Preparation can include developing new sport fabrics such as lycra that enable better movement by players. By preparing in advance how the clothing can be worn in sport it leads to better responses about its effectiveness. The validation of creative ideas in sport is then evaluated based on sales or market performance. Alternatively, when sports fans or players communicate positive thoughts about a creative idea it helps in the development of future products and services.

1.6   Initiative and Sports Entrepreneurship

Sports entrepreneurship requires initiative from individual's organizations and governments who often need to work together. Rank et al. (2004: 523) states personal initiatives include "a range of self-started, proactive and persistent behaviours". This is especially evident in a sports context as initiative is part of the competitive spirit of many games. Rank et al. (2004) suggests the main types of personal initiatives are qualitative, quantitative and overcoming barriers. Qualitative initiatives include going beyond the job description in a way that adds value. In sport this can include helping others improve their plays as being a member of a team. Quantitative initiatives involve spending more energy than required at work in a way that moves forward current practices. Sometimes in sport this quantitative initiative is required to progress in one's career. Overcoming barriers involves persevering in times of hardship. In sport often persistence and belief is the defining characteristic of a resilient athlete or team. Thus, some athletes may retire from an injury only to return when it is healed. Others may change their playing style or consistently enter competitions in the hope that their long term performance will be better. A way to persevere is by challenging past practices by recognizing new ideas are needed. To do this it helps to promote constructive rather than critical comments throughout the development of an innovation.

Sports entrepreneurship can involve a range of activities from experimentation of new ideas to the testing of different production methods. In order to facilitate sports entrepreneurship information needs to be collected and exchanged. Sports organizations can be distinguished from other types of organizations due to their community spirit and basis in society. Many sport organizations have historical and socio-cultural aspects that influence the development of entrepreneurship. This has meant that sports entrepreneurship research has originated in business management and then been adapted to the sports context. There is still a substantial gap about sports entrepreneurship research as sports entrepreneurs are affected by their surroundings, which affect the ability to access market knowledge and funding. Some regions invest more in leisure activities including sport that leads to more entrepreneurial ventures.

Institutions influence the quality of business, cultural and government environments (Dvoultey 2017). There are both formal and informal institutions that affect sport development. Formal institutions try to regulate conduct by reducing transaction costs. Dvoultey (2017: 14) states formal institutions include "regulations, procedures, start-up costs, procedures needed to set up an enterprises, access to credit, taxes". Some countries have more formal sport institutions due to their focus on certain sports. There are also international formal sport institutions that impact entrepreneurship. These include sport governing bodies such as the International Olympic Committee. Informal institutions try to decrease uncertainty in society. Some informal sports institutions are more influential than others depending on the type of sport. Dvoultey (2017: 14) defines informal institutions as "culture, corruption perceptions, attitudes towards entrepreneurs, entrepreneurship perceptions". Thus, sport organizations utilize informal institutions in the form of social capital to access resources.

Ahlstrom and Ding (2014: 614) states that institutional theory suggests "the beliefs, goals and actions of individuals and groups, particularly working in an organizational setting, are shaped by various environmental influences". Entrepreneurial ventures can be constrained or enabled by institutional structures (Ahlstrom and Ding 2014). Some sports institutions limit the freedom of clubs to do new things due to the strict regulations. Other institutions enable sports clubs to change by adopting a proactive strategy. Institutions can be characterized at the macro level in terms of policy and regulation (Ahlstrom and Ding 2014). In sport the professional leagues have rules they need to follow, which can make it hard for them to innovate. Some sports institutions such as the National Basketball Association have had an entrepreneurial sport policy by encouraging internationalization. Institutions at the micro level are concerned with attitudes and individual characteristics (Ahlstrom and Ding 2014). This means that there are expected ways people in sport are supposed to behave. Commitment to entrepreneurship by sports clubs has been growing in recent years.

1.7 Entrepreneurship and Sport: The Link

Entrepreneurship and sport are increasingly being mentioned together. This is due to entrepreneurship impacting economic development and social growth in sport. Schumpeter (1934) was amongst the first to suggest that new ideas are the key to competitiveness. Entrepreneurs play an important role in creating new companies and markets in the sport sector and has transformed many sports organizations by reforming entrenched business practices. Entrepreneurs tend to have specific personality traits of being risk tolerant and able to solve problems. In addition, they are seen as being innovative, proactive and risk taking. It is important to explore the background and characteristics of sports entrepreneurs. This is due to the increased relevance of sport entrepreneurship as a motivation for business creation. Sports entrepreneurs have common traits such as enjoying interacting with the leisure activity. To survive sports entrepreneurs need to be good communicators and actively involved in progressing their business. Sport entrepreneurs make a positive contribution to society by advancing sports-related innovation.

Research on sport and entrepreneurship is a relatively novel field of interest. It is argued that sports entrepreneurship is based on contextual elements and, thus for understanding its workings it is important to follow the ways it is embedded in society. Sport and entrepreneurship have risen as key words in academic, policy and practice discourse because of their affect on the competitiveness of regions. During the last decade, the importance of sport and entrepreneurship has been repeatedly stated by government and business authorities. In addition, the role of sport in society has risen as a competitive strategy to boost regional economies due to its impact on other industry settings. It is not always clear about what sport entrepreneurship includes due to its recent addition to the academic literature. Therefore, sports entrepreneurship can be described as an activity continuum from low to high levels of creativity and innovation in the sports context.

Johannesson (2012) suggests that there are two main features of entrepreneurship. First, there is a capacity to perceive change through the recognition of opportunities. This results in entrepreneurship being a process of adaptation and new ideas that progress to fill a business need in the marketplace. Second, there is an ability to get things done, which is reflected in the need to carry out different forms of action. This book utilizes the broad view of entrepreneurship in a sports context. Thus, the book endorses the view that sports entrepreneurship is the process of getting things done, which involves a realization that it can change depending on the context.

There is a degree of self-action and interaction in entrepreneurship that helps it progress (Johannesson 2012). Self-action means that people come up with ideas from their own volition. An individual's environment may influence this self-action but normally it requires some level of special skills in order for it to come to fruition. Sport entrepreneurs are renowned for their energetic and determined nature that requires discipline in order to develop business ideas. Interaction refers to the social discourse required for ideas to gain momentum in the marketplace (Johannesson 2012). Some entrepreneurs need the feedback from others to move forward with ideas. This is due to the knowledge coming from interactions.

The sport industry has had a significant impact on the international economy through the products and services it provides. The public infrastructure towards sport has risen in conjunction with the increased interest in how it creates new jobs. More people are becoming interested in sport due to its entrepreneurial nature and way it creates opportunities. Sport has both profit and non-profit roles in society that makes it a unique industry. Entrepreneurship in sport has an impact on business success due to more companies becoming interested in the industry.

Sports entrepreneurs utilize alternative ways of doing business to bring about change. This is important as society is changing and there is the realization that new knowledge is required to keep up to date with change. Therefore, sport entrepreneurs need to have a curiosity that enables them to see potential before others. This involves being tenacious and purposeful about the type of entrepreneurship they are doing in the sports context. Some forms of sports entrepreneurship are more societal and community-based such as increasing diversity in existing sports. Other forms are more commercial in nature such as developing new sports that require more stakeholder engagement. Depending on the time and resources required for the sports entrepreneurship new ideas may progress quickly whilst others take time to develop.

Sport entrepreneurs can be opportunity or necessity driven depending on the circumstances. Opportunity driven sport entrepreneurs see a gap in the market to fill by offering a novel product or service. Normally these types of entrepreneurs have another job but see a business potential to add to their existing revenue stream. Necessity driven sport entrepreneurs have to develop new ideas because they are paid to or it is incorporated into their self-employment. This means that they are constantly reviewing the market for new trends or ideas.

1.8   Sport Entrepreneurship as a Research Domain

Sports entrepreneurship has emerged as a research domain at the time more people are interested in leisure, health and wellness activity. The increased interest about sports entrepreneurship has occurred with the rapid introduction of communications technology into the marketplace. In addition, there has been more ways technology is utilized in sport and this has accelerated the use of entrepreneurship. Sports entrepreneurship can be defined as developing new start-ups or ventures that engage with sport. This definition can be broadened to include non-profit and social forms of entrepreneurship that are apparent in sport. A more refined definition of sports entrepreneurship is the exploitation of opportunities within the sports sector to create change. This definition acknowledges that discovery and evaluating entrepreneurship in sport can occur in a variety of ways.

Sports entrepreneurship is an important research area at the intersection of both entrepreneurship and sport. Scholars from a range of disciplines not only from entrepreneurship and sports management are attached to sports entrepreneurship. This includes economic geography, information communications technology, political science, sociology and urban planning due to the impact sport has on these fields. Thus, sport entrepreneurship has high potential to utilize theories both from entrepreneurship and sport in a business setting.

The development of concepts specifically for sports entrepreneurship is a complex process as it requires looking at multiple disciplines. There are different ways of understanding sports entrepreneurship that requires a different explanation. Some knowledge needs to be applied to sports entrepreneurship by tailoring it in a specific way. The use of sports entrepreneurship theory can help build new lines of research inquiry. Therefore, the development of new theories requires a process of refining arguments for a specific context. Sometimes this involves comparing and extending existing theory used in other disciplines. This helps to build the field of sports entrepreneurship by providing a systematic evaluation of its future potential. Moreover, sports entrepreneurship has the distinctive features of (1) incorporating sport as the platform for change and (2) utilizing business purposes for performance. Thus, the sports entrepreneurship literature embraces a wide degree of variability in the types of business activity. The alternative explanations for sports entrepreneurship enable a better understanding of its emergence.

The definition of sports entrepreneurship has evolved from focusing purely on business ventures to extend to opportunity creation processes. This means that the emphasis on sports entrepreneurship is on the discovery of creative ways to move forward the sports field. Therefore, there are a significant number of topical areas under the umbrella of sports entrepreneurship. As sports entrepreneurship continues to evolve there are challenges in keeping sports entrepreneurship as a distinct discipline due to its interdisciplinary nature. This means that there will be tensions about how to continue to work on sports entrepreneurship. Moreover, the field can be distinguished based on its practical and sustainable field of entrepreneurship and sports management. Therefore, sports entrepreneurship needs to continue to absorb other disciplines by focusing on key growth areas. This can occur through a process of discussion about sports entrepreneurship and encourage new research.

Sports organizations face significant competitive challenges in the global economy made more significant by technology change. This has resulted in the need to manage technology whilst developing new products and services. To solve these competitive pressures organizations have advocated entrepreneurship as a way to develop innovative cultures. This can be conducted by organizations recognizing they need to empower employees by rewarding creativity. By helping with problem solving organizations can also create feedback about innovation.

Sports organizations can utilize innovation as a long term benefit to stakeholders. To do this a more supportive organizational environment is needed that formulates ideas them implements them into the marketplace. Creativity is often stifled by bureaucracy and inertia in organizations (Baucus et al. 2008). This means that a more novel way to derive ideas and put them into practice is required. A way to overcome negative patterns towards creativity in organizations in through empowerment. Baucus et al. (2008: 98) suggests there are three attributes of empowerment "employees are given reasonable autonomy; they are provided with mission critical resources; they are given the freedom to fail". Thus, in sports organizations there needs to be some independence in terms of experimenting with new ideas. This can be conducted with strategies aimed at providing time for individuals to dream and formulate action plans. It also is important to realize that there is a trial and error process before success.

This book helps us to understand entrepreneurial processes related to sport and provides insights into the creation of entrepreneurial sports ventures. There is great potential for analyzing sport from an entrepreneurial perspective to inform both the research and practice of sport. The key contribution of this book is to provide a detailed discussion about sports entrepreneurship. To move the sports entrepreneurship literature forward there needs to be more knowledge about the interaction between sport and entrepreneurship.

1.9   Chapters in This Book

This book includes chapters that will provide direction and insight for future sports entrepreneurship research. The book specifically includes chapters that incorporate a cross disciplinary perspective about sports entrepreneurship. This helps to bridge the gap between sports entrepreneurship practice and theory development. There needs to be more consistency in the domain vocabulary about what is involved with sports entrepreneurship. This involves scholars identifying key components of sports entrepreneurship research in order to establish its distinctiveness. There are different approaches to understanding sports entrepreneurship in order to enable the field to be open to alternative explanations. This helps to solve problems occurring in the sports world from an entrepreneurship perspective. New insights from other disciplines can help build the research around sports entrepreneurship.

The aim of this book is to advance research and theory in sports entrepreneurship by utilizing existing literature to integrate it into emerging concepts. This will help to inspire more research into sports entrepreneurship and is intended to serve as a way to develop future research. Each chapter tries to take a thought provoking role in stimulating interest in sports entrepreneurship. This will help to lay a foundation for the sports entrepreneurship discipline. The next chapter discusses how the sport industry affects the development of entrepreneurship. This is important due to the large growth internationally in sport and its inclusion of many different types of innovations and business ventures. The third chapter focuses on sport participation as an entrepreneurial endeavour and how sport can act as a game changer. This is important due to the changing context of sport in society combining both profit and non-profit objectives. Increasingly there is the use of creative marketing and strategies in sport that enable organizations to increase their competitiveness. The fourth chapter examines the role of athlete entrepreneurs and their importance for entrepreneurship. Many athletes and other stakeholders become sport entrepreneurs due to their experience and emotional attachment to sport so this chapter is helpful in understanding the connection. In addition, more athletes after their professional career has finished start up businesses related to sport. This has led to innovations occurring both in the business and sport sector from athlete-based business endeavours. The fifth chapter focuses on different perspectives of innovation in sport, which is needed for sport entrepreneurship. As innovation can take a variety of forms, the chapter discusses how the sport context influences innovation capacity. Sport entrepreneurship can occur in a planned manner through the use of resources in an innovative manner. However, there can also be unplanned forms of entrepreneurship that happen by chance or through serendipity. The sixth chapter discusses how to envision change in sport by focusing on the business aspects. This is useful as the concept of sport is altering due to electronic gaming and other technology trends. There has been a growing recognition in the international business world about the role sport plays in commercial and social activities. The seventh chapter focuses on systems and entrepreneurial ecosystems in sport, which are helpful in creating a conducive environment for change. The system processes in sport entrepreneurship need to be understood as a way to harness the potential of change in the sport context. The eighth chapter notes the role of ethics in sport. Community and corporate social responsibility initiatives in a sport context are stated, which are part of sport ethics. Increasingly there is more interest in sport ethics as it influences playing conditions and standards of behavior. However, due to emerging technology and innovation there needs to be more link between ethics and sport entrepreneurship, which is the reason for the focus on the interlinkages. Chapter 9 then discusses the role education and policy is playing in sport entrepreneurship. Educational institutions have different perceptions about how they integrate sport into the pedagogy, service and research activities. Higher education institutions have focused on sport as a source of revenue, which impacts the management of policy initiatives. Lastly, chapter 10 discusses the future for sport entrepreneurship and the contribution of this book. The complex nature of sports entrepreneurship means that it is multi-disciplinary and draws upon emerging research areas. I hope this book will stimulate more dialogue about sports entrepreneurship.

1.10   Conclusion

The aim of this chapter has been to review the development of sport entrepreneurship as a unique field of study. The way sport and entrepreneurship are combined in the literature was discussed that highlights the novelty of sports entrepreneurship. Research on sports entrepreneurship will yield important contributions to the literature. Sport entrepreneurship is an exciting area for research as there are many opportunities to contribute to conceptual and empirical breakthroughs. The purpose of this chapter is to provoke thought about the role of entrepreneurship in sport. More attention will be given to the evolutionary development of sports entrepreneurship. In this chapter, I attempted to address the paucity of literature on entrepreneurship in sport. By focusing on the linkage between sport and entrepreneurship I am moving forward the literature on this area. Despite the many examples of entrepreneurship in sport there is still a lack of research about this field, which is the reason for this book. The following chapters will discuss in more detail specific topics related to sports entrepreneurship.

References

Ahlstrom, D., & Ding, Z. (2014). Entrepreneurship in China: An overview. *International Small Business Journal, 32*(6), 610–618.

Baucus, M. S., Norton, W. I., Baucus, D. A., & Human, S. E. (2008). Fostering creativity and innovation without encouraging unethical behaviour. *Journal of Business Ethics, 81*, 97–115.

Dvoultey, O. (2017). Determinants of Nordic entrepreneurship. *Journal of Small Business and Enterprise Development, 24*(1), 12–33.

Hemphill, D. (2005). Cybersport. *Journal of the Philosophy of Sport, 32*, 195–207.

Hjalager, A. (2010). A review of innovation research in tourism. *Tourism Management, 31*, 1–12.

Jenny, S. E., Manning, R. D., Keiper, M. C., & Olrich, T. W. (2016). Virtual(ly) athletes: Where eSports fit within the definition of "sport". *Quest, 1*, 1–18.

Johannesson, G. T. (2012). 'To get things done': A relational approach to entrepreneurship. *Scandinavian Journal of Hospitality and Tourism, 1*, 1–16.

Johannesson, J. A., Olsen, B., & Lumpkin, G. T. (2001). Innovation as newness: What is new, how new, and new to whom? *European Journal of Innovation Management, 4*(1), 20–31.

Miragaia, D. A., Ferreira, J., & Ratten, V. (2017). Corporate social responsibility and social entrepreneurship: Drivers of sports sponsorship policy. *International Journal of Sport Policy and Politics, 9*(4), 613–623.

Rank, J., Pace, V. L., & Frese, M. (2004). Three avenues for future research on creativity, innovation and initiative. *Applied Psychology: An International Review, 53*(4), 518–528.

Ratten, V. (2010). Developing a theory of sport-based entrepreneurship. *Journal of Management & Organization, 16*(04), 557–565.

Ratten, V. (2011). Sport-based entrepreneurship: Towards a new theory of entrepreneurship and sport management. *International Entrepreneurship and Management Journal, 7*(1), 57–69.

Ratten, V. (2012). Sport entrepreneurship: Challenges and directions for future research. *International Journal of Entrepreneurial Venturing, 4*(1), 65–76.

Ratten, V. (2017a). *Sports innovation management*. London: Routledge.

Ratten, V. (2017b). Entrepreneurial sport policy. *International Journal of Sport Policy and Politics, 9*(4), 641–648.

Ratten, V., & Babiak, K. (2010). The role of social responsibility, philanthropy and entrepreneurship in the sport industry. *Journal of Management & Organization, 16*(04), 482–487.

Ratten, V., & Ratten, H. (2011). International sport marketing: Practical and future research implications. *Journal of Business & Industrial Marketing, 26*(8), 614–620.

Schumpeter, J. (1934). *The theory of economic development*. Cambridge: Harvard University Press.

Solvoll, S., Alsos, G. A., & Bulanova, O. (2015). Tourism entrepreneurship – Review and future directions. *Scandinavian Journal of Hospitality and Tourism, 15*(1), 120–137.

The Sport Industry and Entrepreneurship

2

2.1 Introduction

Sport is one of the largest and fastest growing industries in the world. Most aspects of sport from changes to challenges affecting the industry can be studied as forms of entrepreneurship. Phan et al. (2010: 175) states that "in the business disciplines, research in entrepreneurship distinguishes itself by its concern with the interactions between individuals, processes and institutions in the emergence of new organizations, and new organizational forms that create economic wealth". Sports can be classified as mainstream or non-mainstream according to its popularity and also newness. Mainstream sports are better known amongst the public for the teams and athletes that are involved in the games. Typical mainstream sports include football and tennis as they have been played for a long time and are usually popular regardless of geographic location. In addition, mainstream sports have players that can become celebrities due to their skills in the game and popularity off the field. Non-mainstream sports are typically less accessible due to the costs involved or knowledge about the sport. This has meant that there is a degree of edginess towards non-mainstream sports as they are played in a different way or involve a different demographic group.

Entrepreneurship is embedded in this history and evolution of the sport industry. To understand the future of sport there needs to be more attention placed on entrepreneurship. This includes improving the incentives for sports entrepreneurship. In addition, sport provides a valuable way for entrepreneurship to be applied, which this chapter will discuss. Sport entrepreneurs are often motivated by lifestyle reasons such as improved quality of life and the pursuit of personal happiness. However, the sport industry in terms of its structure influences the way lifestyle entrepreneurs form businesses as a way to earn a comfortable living but in line with their personal beliefs.

This chapter will discuss the uniqueness of the sport industry and its development in terms of entrepreneurship. The history and review of the sport industry is motivated by there being a lack of understanding about what impacts sport as an entrepreneurial endeavour. Current work on sports entrepreneurship is fragmented

© Springer International Publishing AG 2018
V. Ratten, *Sport Entrepreneurship*, Management for Professionals,
https://doi.org/10.1007/978-3-319-73010-3_2

and lacking in rich discussion about how it contributes to the more general entrepreneurship theory. Thus, there is a need for more clarity about what is distinctive about sports entrepreneurship as a way to move the field forward. More scholars need to focus on how the sport industry influences entrepreneurship as way to identify how it is a unifying framework for both sport and entrepreneurship scholars. This will help to establish the distinctiveness of the sport entrepreneurship discipline.

2.2 Sport

Sport is different to a game as it normally involves some degree of physical activity and overcoming another opponent. This means that physical fitness and ability is important in sport and helps to distinguish it from other activities. In sport, there is deliberate physical action that enables an athlete to manipulate themselves to win a game. This helps in terms of rewarding physical skill to transfer it from being a leisure activity to a sport. It helps to maintain skills in both a strategic and tactical sense in order to play sport. Strategic skill is seeing what the other opponent is doing and beating them at a game.

Some strategies will depend on the type of sport such as the ability to foresee plays being important in football but having knowledge of the water necessary in surfing. For team sports the strategies will differ and often they are planned before the game. Strategies can be physical or psychological depending on the type of sport. For endurance sports such as long distance running the physical strategies might include limiting one's energy until the end of the race or when it is most needed. The psychological strategies will be more in terms of staying positive in times of hardship and pushing oneself towards a goal.

Sport psychology is an interesting part of the game and has become more important in recent times. This has meant that athletes are using visualization and other techniques to see where they want to be in terms of performance. The term sporting intelligence refers to how athletes utilize their skills but also knowledge to make the best performance. Sometimes perseverance rather than skill is important in obtaining the greatest result. Thus, preempting their moves and thinking about future courses of action are important ways of being the best in sport. Some sports people have utilized their sporting intelligence both as a player but also as a coach. This is reflected in many previous tennis stars becoming coaches because of the psychological edge they give players. The sporting intelligence also includes creativity on the field that enables the winning of the game. This can include problem solving skills that allow for athletes or teams to come up with ways to win in times of hardship and success. Thus, both physical skill and strategy are important in sports games.

The most popular sports such as football tend to use physical features such as height and weight as part of the game. In the United States, football is a contact sport and players were protective clothing. However, recently there has been attention placed on head injuries in football and the resulting long term damage.

Football in other countries can also be a contact sport such as that played in Australia but the rules and conduct of the game are different to elsewhere in the world. Football can also mean soccer in many countries and is a non-contact sport depending on the geographic location. It is interesting though that various forms of football such as rugby and soccer are played differently according to country setting and these different forms of the game have tended not to be internationalized. Other sports such as basketball have globalized but distinct forms of football are still largely culturally biased.

Entrepreneurs are praised in the sporting community for their contribution to the development of new products and services. This has led to more business and government attention about how to promote entrepreneurship in sport. Some policies have been introduced that focus on knowledge collaboration as a way to increase innovation and help develop businesses. However, it can be hard to determine the effects of entrepreneurship on sport as there may be a time lag between the development of ideas and the successful implementation of the innovation. This means that there needs to be a continual stream of innovations in sport that lead to more entrepreneurial business ventures to emerge. Most of the benefits of sport entrepreneurship are generated by a small number of highly innovative firms and individuals. This is linked to what Schumpeter (1934) first coined as creative destruction, which occurs with the constant birth and death of new firms. This creative destruction is seen in sport as there is experimentation that occurs naturally from the playing of the game and in some cases enables new ideas.

Sport is usually played in a regular season with weekly games. There are a large number of different sports that range in how they are played to the number of players involved in the competition. Sport is generally defined as a system of activities that involves some form of physical excursion or mental activity. In addition, there are normally customs or standards of behavior that exist in sport, which affect how it is played. This means that there is a degree of subjectivity about appropriate moral behavior about what is right in the sports context. There are rules in sport but this is supplemented by codes of conduct, which reflect appropriate behavior.

Sport normally has objective measures of performance in terms of scoring a goal or having the best performance. Although these measures can be subjective as there is a degree of artistic evaluation in how they are judged. This artistry is becoming more evident in new sports that have grown in conjunction with lifestyle events such as surfing. In most sports the performance is determined by the highest score, which is an objective evaluation. However, this can be influenced by technical indicators that are combined with artistic ability, which occurs in the case of gymnastics.

Sport is one of the oldest pastimes in society and is critical to the healthy functioning of a society. In the past sport was considered a leisure activity and there were more amateurs than professionals although this is changing in society. The term sport is sometimes referred to as leisure or recreational activities depending on the environment. The main characteristic of sport is in the competition as players challenge each other in order to have the best performance. Sport can utilize individual physical activity or forms of technology for competition. This includes the use of cars or animals as part of the sport. Car racing is a popular sport, which is dependent on the technological innovations of the motor racing industry. Horse racing is also popular in addition to greyhound racing that uses animals.

The key benefits of sport are in the physical activity but also mental well-being. In the past there was more manual labour but this has changed with the service economy so people in sedentary or office jobs utilize sport in a different way. Social relationships are a key part of sport and this is a form of networking that helps build better community spirits. However, there are more individual sports that have become popular in recent years due to the more individualistic nature of society. This includes aerobics and yoga, which are conducted in groups but focus on individual performance. In addition, some sports have different categories according to gender and weight that make competition a more even playing field. This is reflected in some sports being based on the best performance or be judged through a committee who decides who was the best player. This occurs in sports such as boxing and gymnastics that has scores for performance from a number of people on the judging committee.

Sport is global but there is a degree of sentimentality around local, regional and national teams. This has resulted in people having a passion for specific teams based on their nationality or location. This is seen in the popularity of sportswear for these teams but also the flow on effects of the participation. Sport has become more professionalized in recent years with more athletes solely focusing on their sports career. This is particularly evident in well-known sports such as football and tennis that have a high degree of prize money that enables players to live off their winnings. Other sports are less professional and this is usually due to smaller sized prize money being offered. Some sports have age restrictions that impact on the time a player becomes a professional athlete. This is seen in the National Football League in the United States, with many athletes playing collegiate football then going into the professional league.

2.3   Sports Industry

The sports industry has stimulated the growth of many small businesses including those in related areas such as tourism and hospitality. There are a number of reasons for the high number of small businesses in the sport industry including: (1) the low overall capital required to start a business, (2) the lack of lengthy training and educational requirements and (3) flexibility of hours and time worked. There is also a trend towards more people becoming professional trainers and lifestyle choices in the sport area. This is due to an increased interest in work/life balance and the desire to be involved in health activity. In addition, there has been the emergence of professional sports training courses because of the desire of more people to be in this business. Most of the training is on coaching styles and less on business ventures, which has created a gap in the industry.

There are three major components of the sport industry: direct suppliers, support services and development agencies. Direct suppliers involve those that are visible in the sport industry and are considered essential elements of the economic ecosystem. This includes sport clubs, clothing companies and television networks. Support services are those that link to direct suppliers by offering additional business. For example, sport magazines, online gaming and food companies. The development agencies are normally related to government service providers or involve educational institutions.

There has been a significant increased interest in the sport and associated industries such as health and fitness. This provides good opportunities but also potential for sport businesses to generate additional income by acting entrepreneurially. There are a number of supporting sectors of the sport industry that are dependent on the entrepreneurial business ventures coming from sport. Thus, more time and energy needs to be spent on entrepreneurial activity. This is due to there being both push and pull factors that influence people to start a business (Glancey and Pettigrew 1997). The push factors include individuals requiring work due to unemployment so they create their own businesses. Jafar et al. (2011: 829) states there are multiple pull factors for starting a business and these include "providing employment for family members, generating additional income, meeting the need of the market, companionship with guests, fulfilling their interest or hobby, and providing employment to communities". In many countries after financial crises individuals start businesses as a form of income but also as a necessity in times of economic hardship. The pull factors include lifestyle reasons and desire to control one's own destiny. This means that many individuals start businesses due to opportunities they perceive in the marketplace.

Sport entrepreneurs utilize the instability of the industry to identify emerging trends. This requires a change in thinking about potential business opportunities as a way to evolve the sports industry. Sport entrepreneurs can be described as those who see an opportunity to develop a related business venture. This means that there is a need to be creative in order to utilize environmental changes as a way to develop sport entrepreneurship. The key attribute of a sports entrepreneur is in their ability to take risks and see new trends. Sometimes this requires a period of hardship whilst the business is growing in order to develop key skills in this area.

Most sport entrepreneurs need to have confidence that what they are doing is correct and will have a benefit in the long-term. Some sport business owners have not been receptive to future trends and avoided entrepreneurial endeavours due to the perception of risk. This has meant that the sport entrepreneurs that tend to do well recognize failure is part of business but that they can learn from experience. Thus, more sport business owners have been willing to engage in calculated risks as a way to understand potential opportunities.

The sport industry has generally been supportive of entrepreneurship as it provides a way to move the field forward. The culture in sport can be considered entrepreneurial due to the positive attitudes towards innovation and change. Sport entrepreneurs act as agents of change to build creativity within an industry renowned for its competitiveness. The sport industry attracts entrepreneurship due to the low barriers to entry and ability to contribute to performance. There are sport industry specific entrepreneurial behaviors that impact investment. This is related to the cultural context of sport that is dependent on organizational behavior. Often sport entrepreneurs mix business and personal objectives to derive business ideas.

There are specific sport industry characteristics that play a role in the development of businesses, thus, it is crucial that more attention be placed on how to recognize and nurture sport entrepreneurship. In the sports industry, there tends to be more social capital due to the connection between individuals and business owners in partnership with government entities. There is also a perception in the sport industry that it is desirable to be entrepreneurial due to the need for a progression of ideas and innovation. In addition, in a sport context, entrepreneurship is often a strategic objective due to its ability to exploit opportunities within different industries.

2.4   Entrepreneurship in Sport

Entrepreneurship is significantly influenced by the extent of innovation and creativity within an industry environment (Anggadwita et al. 2016). For entrepreneurship to develop it needs to be sustained through the continual education and feedback of important information. This involves consistently developing a good environment for creativity so that organizations feel confident in the entrepreneurship process. For some it may involve sport managers improvising on required resources until they are available. This can include an orientation towards entrepreneurship as part of company life. Moreover, there needs to be a realization that some industries have more expectations about entrepreneurship. In the sport industry, there is usually a significant amount of government funding that can help with the acquisition and allocation of resources. To help build entrepreneurship sport managers need to institute appropriate practices that encourage novel ideas and procedures such as forecasting future trends and brainstorming about potential products and services.

Entrepreneurship is a way to enhance growth and thus create more prosperous sport businesses and organizations. Entrepreneurship provides a way to facilitate technological development that is often the source of competitive advantage in sport. To maintain the competitive advantage of businesses in sport there needs to be a constant lookout for ways of being entrepreneurial that enable increased economic performance. This means involving entrepreneurs who are responsible for producing change and innovation in sport. However, entrepreneurship can also be embedded in the economic and social ecosystem of sport and it enables co-creation and facilitates change.

Entrepreneurship usually involves the creation of a business entity but can also be involved in the opening of new markets, reorganizing of existing organizational structures and the production of new goods. For this reason, it is important that sport entities focus on how they can access new ideas that enable better resource usage of materials for innovative purposes. Entrepreneurship in sport can take a variety of processes from within firms, to between institutions and government bodies that alter the way innovation develops. There are also the policy sides of entrepreneurship that provide important guidelines for how innovation is produced in a sport context. Thus, it is important to understand how entrepreneurship is embedded in the processes of sport by providing knowledge that can help future policy makers and practitioners. Moreover, there is also entrepreneurship within sport derived from the experiences people have about the role of change in a sporting context. This helps to gain knowledge about the meanings of sport entrepreneurship in terms of how it is evolving as a business discipline.

More studies about sport are realizing that the process of sport is entrepreneurial. This has meant that there is now more research on how entrepreneurship can be applied to sports. Consequently, the concepts of sport and entrepreneurship have gained an increased attention in the literature. Entrepreneurship often takes place in sports organizations as spin offs from marketing and sponsorship activities. This is due to the specific role entrepreneurship has in the sports ecosystem.

There is little accumulated knowledge about the role of sport and entrepreneurship due to the relative newness of the field. Sport entrepreneurship is an interdisciplinary subject that can be studied from a number of different disciplines and perspectives. This makes sport entrepreneurship research an important emerging research area that bridges the gap between practice and theory. However, the research has considerable heterogeneity due to the large number of different types of entrepreneurship in sport. The main ways entrepreneurship is embedded in sport is as an output, process or discourse. As an output it means new businesses, products, services or technologies that are developed in the sport context. As a process it involves coming up with new ways to get services to consumers and as a discourse it involves discussion about potential future products.

The contribution of sport to the economy cannot be ignored as it is part of the social fabric of society. Entrepreneurship is still largely disregarded in sport business research and there is a gap in the field. Sport is mostly presented in the literature as an activity that involves physical use of the human body or in an electronic way as a form of competition. Entrepreneurship influences sport organizations through their vision and strategy. Thus, a new understanding of sport entrepreneurship interactions is needed to address emerging research areas. The existing literature about entrepreneurship tends to view it as a profit or non-profit form without stressing the industry context of the process. This has meant entrepreneurship specifically dealing with sport has been left behind as more studies focus on the type of entrepreneurship rather than the industry. In sport there are a number of possible ways entrepreneurship can be utilized in terms of understanding both individual, firm and industry behavior. Typically entrepreneurs in sport are considered as outside entities that go into the sport context rather than being embedded in the industry ecosystem. This has undermined the existing and potential contribution that athletes, players, coaches and fans have made to the way entrepreneurship develops in a sports context.

Entrepreneurship is considered as being open to anyone that has an idea but sometimes it is limited by availability of resources. This is due to time scarcity and financial funding affecting the way ideas are progressed in sport. Many entrepreneurs overcome these limitations due to their ambition and drive that makes them successful in the marketplace. In recent decades there has been a change in the number of new ideas entering the sports industry due to technological change. This has meant that there are more opportunities for ideas to progress in sport that integrate technology, which can help improve competitiveness.

Sport entrepreneurship involves both a process and an outcome. The process concerns how the entrepreneurship develops by an individual or organization. The outcome is about the results from the entrepreneurial process. It is helpful to include both the process and outcome of sports entrepreneurship as it enables a better explanation of the factors involved. This helps to simultaneously foster sports entrepreneurship that can add value for all stakeholders. Sports entrepreneurship can involve surprising ideas that seem unrealistic but work in practice. This means that some ideas for sports entrepreneurship are dramatically different to what has been done before. To be successful though the idea needs to work well in the sports context otherwise it will not have market appeal. Entrepreneurship is embedded in most sports contexts but not all.

Some sports organizations are naturally entrepreneurial but others need to work at being considered as innovative. There may be contextual factors involved including technology changes that make some sports organizations more entrepreneurial than others. Entrepreneurship does not require a special way of doing business but is rather a mindset. There is some anecdotal evidence in the sports industry that entrepreneurship is considered a necessity. This is due to entrepreneurship being a positive attribute that increase both financial and non-financial performance. More sports organizations are encouraging educational processes about entrepreneurship. This means that entrepreneurship education helps build a system that enables network building and information exchange. Sometimes there is a hotbed of entrepreneurship in sport but it needs to be capitalized in order to be developed.

2.5 Multidisciplinary Background for Sport Entrepreneurship

Alves et al. (2007: 30) states that a multidisciplinary and multisectoral cooperative environment involves "settings, formal or informal, that bring together organizations from different entrepreneurial sectors and science and technology institutions around common goals". Sport is a good example of a multidisciplinary environment as there are both private and non-profit entities that contribute to the industry. This is evident in the need to use public funds to support sports facilities that are then staffed by private organizations. In sport there is also research and development in terms of science and medicine that are integral parts of the industry. As the leisure industry that incorporates sport has more attention placed on it due to the aging population but also general increased interest in health topics there is a need to bridge together more stakeholders. This is important in fostering entrepreneurship in the multidisciplinary sport environment that prides itself on its international appeal and emotional attachment to communities. In sport there are diverse knowledge skills needed to enable the sport system to grow and develop. This is due to a variety of sports being played in different geographic contexts that are important in fostering innovative behavior. This can led to creativity in terms of how knowledge leads to the development of technological sport products and processes. Some sports focus on technology for their competitiveness and this is evident in the amount of money they spend on research.

Alves et al. (2007) states that cooperative multidisciplinary environments have three core dimensions: diversity, coherence and interactivity. Diversity is in terms of the different strengths and weaknesses of sport entities in the environment. Some sport organizations might be better at marketing that enable the growth of a region as a distinct place. This helps with creating both private and public sports entities that can work on projects of a mutual interest. There will be sport entities that have distinct competences that enable them to enter the marketplace at a faster rate, which can enable related entities to piggyback from their success. This enables a more level playing field that fosters entrepreneurship at the local, community, regional and international level of sport. Coherence involves having complementary sport activities that foster mutually beneficial results. For many sports there is a requirement of a playing field or facility that works with athletes in order to create the right environment. This means that knowledge can be spilled over to other sporting entities when they work in a productive manner. Interactivity involves the cooperative relationships existing between various members of a sports community. In professional sports there needs to be cooperation between the sports venue, media and fans in order to bring about the best environment. This requires time and skills in managing cooperative relationships.

A process perspective to understanding sport entrepreneurship is needed to advance the research on this area. This enables a broader perspective about entrepreneurship in sport as a way to legitimize sports entrepreneurship. It is helpful to understand the processes of sport entrepreneurship in order to reproduce and add new insights. Some entrepreneurship in sport has remained invisible due to fast changing nature of the sport industry. Much of the entrepreneurship in sport is assumed rather than planned, which makes it difficult to ascertain. For this reason, sport is a highly entrepreneurial industry and is a both a source and consequence of the competitiveness.

Existing research on entrepreneurship is not sufficient to explain the processes in sport. This means that there is a need to understand the processes of entrepreneurship in sport in order to increase theory development and encourage more empirical research. Some entrepreneurship is a result of social expectations in sport that facilitate communication and dissemination of information. This means that the socialization process in sport will encourage more entrepreneurship that leads to change. Furthermore, entrepreneurship in sport should be explored more by understanding the different process perspectives. It is important that there is more awareness of the entrepreneurship in sport. This is due to entrepreneurship being needed to optimize resources usage and to increase the innovation capability of sport.

Entrepreneurship involves purposeful change normally associated with new businesses but can also involve adoption of innovative ideas (Farinha et al. 2017). Sport entrepreneurship is associated with an attitude to imagine something different to what is currently being conducted. This involves new ideas that optimize better delivery of services or produce more efficient outputs. This is a result of sport entrepreneurship involving disrupting current behavior by progressing new ideas. Often this includes changing entrenched patterns to increase better outputs.

Sport entrepreneurship is a philosophy that can be utilized to progress new ideas within the industry. The entrepreneurial climate in the sport industry is growing and becoming a stimulant for business activity. However, there can be some negative aspects of the sport industry that hinder the development of an entrepreneurial climate. This includes a culture of teams and consensus decision making rather than individual freedom. There is also a reliance on government funding to support sport that means there is a lack of incentive to be independently funded. In addition, there can be a reliance on institutional structures rather than the focusing on new linkages and interests.

The contextual embeddedness of sports entrepreneurship provides a way to understand its development. There needs to be new direction in sport entrepreneurship research to advance current thinking and to solidify its position within business management studies. This includes appreciating the cultural background of sport, which encourages a move towards new ways of thinking about sport entrepreneurship. Entrepreneurship has been studied from a range of disciplines but only recently from a sports perspective. Most studies on entrepreneurship focus on businesses in the manufacturing sector with less emphasis on the sport industry.

The process of entrepreneurship in sport is complex and involves launching new businesses through the introduction of innovation (Ratten 2012). Normally entrepreneurship will begin with the recognition of an opportunity, which then requires an evaluation of the resources to implement the idea. The resources include venture capital and start up financing, which need to be conducted before the idea moves into the commercialization phase (Ratten 2013). The sport industry is fragmented into different types of businesses. There are special circumstances in sport that drive entrepreneurship. This includes location, governance structure and type of sport so it is important to highlight the importance of entrepreneurship in sport by assuming it is a natural occurrence. Entrepreneurship is a mechanism that increases the competitiveness of the sport industry. The competitive environment of sport can help explain the incidence and prevalence of entrepreneurship.

The discovery process in entrepreneurship involves the formation of beliefs that a gap exists in the marketplace (Phan et al. 2010). This means that resources need to be devoted to the process of making the discovery a reality. New insights and creativity are part of the discovery process, which influences new business ventures (Ratten 2014). Creativity in a business setting is different to that occurring in an artistic environment due to the need for both novelty and usefulness (Phan et al. 2010). In business, creativity needs to have a practical value in order for it to be significant.

Sport entrepreneurs are motivated to establish new ventures based on their economic and social context. This means that to be a successful entrepreneur there needs to be decisions made based on knowledge about market potential (Ratten 2014). In the sports context there is often a strong bond amongst members of the entrepreneur's social network. This means there are some business obligations based on being a member of a social network. Normally more trust develops when there is a reciprocity in exchange relationships (Ratten and Dana 2017). Sport entrepreneurs can use their social networks as a source of information in terms of building their entrepreneurial success. In addition, there is more information that can be exchanged through these social networks that leads to better entrepreneurial performance. This means that the more an entrepreneur can coordinate their networks the better the likely result (Ratten and Tajeddini 2017). It is important to have a consensus about the role of entrepreneurship in sport as it helps to build knowledge. The government has a role in triggering entrepreneurship as it helps to create new jobs and economic opportunities (Ratten 2017).

Sports entrepreneurship is a specific type of entrepreneurship whose participants are motivated by conducting business related to sport and is multi-layered because it involves different dimensions from social, technological and international. Entrepreneurship is a wide concept dominated by cultural, economic and social dimensions that are embedded in an environmental context. Gaining an understanding of sport entrepreneurship has important implications for policy and practice. This is due to sport entrepreneurs having direct implications on other industry segments.

Entrepreneurship involves "the act of directing resources (financial and physical) in new ways for the generation of profit" (Shinde 2010: 524). The core characteristics of sport entrepreneurs are having initiative and wanting to create a business. Behavioral attitudes are also important for the growth of sport entrepreneurs who combine their managerial capabilities in a creative way. For entrepreneurship to grow there needs to be a supportive environment that expects positive outcomes (Ratten et al. 2017).

The articulation of entrepreneurship in sport can be difficult due to the lack of direct consensus about what is innovative. This means that sports entrepreneurship is modified based on cultural conditions. It is known that sport entrepreneurship is increasing due to technological advances and a general global trend towards health and wellness activities. Entrepreneurship is affecting most aspects of the sport industry especially in related sectors such as leisure and tourism. There are innovations in sport occurring at a rapid rate that were previously not considered as viable. Examples of these innovations include online sports technology startups or apps that interact with customers. These sport apps give users scores and statistics about their performance enabling them more access to knowledge.

Some consider sport as entrepreneurship as it involves people working on a specific purpose in a competitive environment. This means that being part of the sport industry is helpful in maintaining an entrepreneurial mindset. Sport like business is about the creation and maintenance of relationships for a specific purpose. These relationships involve people working on different aspects of the business from playing a sport to refereeing the game to being a spectator.

There is a passion in sport that differentiates it from other industries. Thus, there is ample opportunity for entrepreneurship in different segments of the sport industry from equipment manufacturing to the development of new online services. Some of the highest growth sports businesses have been around digital and social media. This is due to the desire for people to experience sport in new ways based on technological advancements. More people are seeing sport not just as a form of physical activity but also as a mental stimulation due to the increased usage of electronic games. Gaining an understanding of sport entrepreneurship has important implications for managers. This is due to sports entrepreneurship being a combination of innovation, risk taking and foresight that needs persistence to achieve its outcomes. A useful way to understand sports entrepreneurship is to separate it into sport and entrepreneurship.

A sport entrepreneur is a person who shows creativity in bringing together resources in a new way that creates a business venture. Some sport entrepreneurs are interested solely in financial profits but others see themselves as part of the community and have social goals. In addition, there has been a new climate emerging in sport due to the search for new objectives based around new trends. New technology has fuelled entrepreneurship in sport due to the business implications. This technological change has helped revive some sports that were going out of fashion by providing new playing methods. It has also transformed sports by providing additional virtual places that sport can be played.

2.6   Foresight and Sport

Konnola et al. (2007: 608) states "foresight activities have often provided support for objectives such as priority-setting, networking and consensual vision-building". Foresight is important in evaluating potential opportunities around sports entrepreneurship. In the sport industry, there is sometimes a high level of uncertainty caused by new technological innovations entering the marketplace. This means that foresight can help with making ideas more action-orientated so that they have a better potential of being used in the marketplace. This enables sports organizations to stay focused on potential innovations that will have a positive contribution to their industry. Often a way to encourage better foresight is to have a group of ideas that can be used as a form of portfolio management. This means the acknowledgement that some ideas will be successful but not others depending on how they progress. Ideas need to be generated in the sport industry to encourage new ways of thinking to emerge. However, these ideas need to be revised based on feedback and iterations until they have been implemented into the marketplace. It is useful to use new ideas about sport as a way to encourage the development of entrepreneurial strategies.

As sport entities are often embedded in a stakeholder network it helps to build a common vision in order to effectively manage resources. This means that the entrepreneurial ecosystem in sport can develop based on the adaptability of ideas. Konnola et al. (2007: 609) suggests that a way to encourage foresight in innovation is through diversity, which they define as "the condition or quality of being diverse, different or varied". The concepts of diversity and innovation are similar as they both acknowledge the importance of new and different ways of thinking. In addition, the process of entrepreneurship in sport is characterized by diversity and innovation. This helps to exploit opportunities for the potential they bring into the marketplace. Ideas can be co-created with stakeholders in sport that bridge the gap between theory and practice. It is important to anticipate changes in sport by scanning the market for future trends. A way to do this is by analyzing innovative ideas by systematically evaluating their potential. As sport combines public and private entities it helps to have a co-creation process that builds on mutual commenting. This enables the building of prospective ideas by exploring ways to develop innovation. Sometimes these ideas are distributed through innovation systems that encourage a discussion to develop.

The goal of sports entrepreneurship is to embrace change by creating new value networks that link together previous structures with new innovation systems. To be effective the innovation needs to prioritize goals and objectives in order to give attention to the most effective ideas. This involves focusing on networking in sport to utilize existing resources but also develop new capabilities. In addition, there can be alternative ways to progress innovations in sport but this might involve challenging existing structures. This is due to there being political systems that may favour the status quo rather than innovation. Stakeholders in sport can be proactive about developing innovation by envisioning alternative approaches. This includes reducing uncertainty by managing risk in an appropriate way. Some sports innovations may need more start-up capital whilst others naturally evolve in the market. Therefore, it is important for sports organizations to explore alternative ways of developing ideas that have the ability to strengthen market potential.

As part of developing innovative ideas in sport, the market needs to be evaluated for signals about approaching trends. Konnola et al. (2007: 611) suggest that weak signals are "new, surprising, uncertain, irrational, not credible, difficult to track down, related to a substantial time lag before maturing and becoming mainstream". It is sometimes hard for people to gauge early indicators of potentially lucrative new ideas in sport. This is due to the difficulty or reluctance of people to share information and disseminate knowledge. Some innovations are dependent on demand by consumers but also the obtaining of regulatory approval. Other innovations will require a substantial amount of investment that makes it necessary to gain support from governments and business entities. Communication channels including online social media help disseminate ideas and spread information about potential new trends. This is due to there being a need to recognise in these communication channels that collaboration may be required to build the innovations. It helps to have social interaction between different stakeholders in a sport context in order to develop concepts. Ideas to progress should be commented on by participants as a way of elaborating potential new course of action.

2.7   Conclusion

This chapter proved the importance of the sport industry context to the development of sports entrepreneurship. As there are an abundance of small businesses in the sport industry it is important to highlight the role of entrepreneurship. I aspire to make several contributions to the entrepreneurship field of study by including a sport perspective. By integrating the sport and entrepreneurship literature, I demonstrate the overlapping research areas. This means that there is a need to foster entrepreneurship in business that involves sport. Sport entrepreneurs usually have specific characteristics that distinguish them from other types of entrepreneurs. This includes the desire to be involved with sport due to lifestyle and emotional attachments. To survive in the spots industry, more small business owners need to think and act entrepreneurially. This includes reaching out to new markets but also embracing emerging technological innovations. Many sport businesses utilize low levels of technology whilst others are dependent on integrating knowledge from other sources. It would be beneficial for more sport businesses to promote entrepreneurial skills development in order to attract more funding. Governments need to work with sport business owners in providing advice and training. This will help them develop talent but also stay at the forefront of the sport industry. As many sport businesses are service-orientated there also needs to be an emphasis on service innovation. Sometimes this can include marketing of new innovations that impact competitiveness. In conclusion, this chapter has discussed the importance of the sport industry for the development of sport entrepreneurship.

References

Alves, J., Marques, M. J., Saur, I., & Marques, P. (2007). Creativity and innovation through multidisciplinary and multisectoral cooperation. *Creativity and Innovation Management, 16* (1), 27–34.

Anggadwita, G., Ramadani, V., Luturlean, B., & Ratten, V. (2016). Socio-cultural environments and emerging economy entrepreneurship: Women entrepreneurs in Indonesia. *Journal of Entrepreneurship in Emerging Economies, 9*(1): 85–96. FOR Code 1503.

Farinha, L., Ferreira, J., Nunes, S., & Ratten, V. (2017). Conditions supporting entrepreneurship and sustainable growth. *International Journal of Social Ecology and Sustainable Development, 8*(3), 67–86.

Glancey, K., & Pettigrew, M. (1997). Entrepreneurship in the small hotel sector. *International Journal of Contemporary Hospitality Management, 9*(1), 1.

Jafar, M., Abdul-Aziz, A. R., Maideen, S. A., & Mohd, S. Z. (2011). Entrepreneurship in the tourism industry: Issues in developing countries. *International Journal of Hospitality Management, 30*, 827–835.

Konnola, T., Brummer, V., & Salo, A. (2007). Diversity in foresight: Insights form the fostering of innovation ideas. *Technological Forecasting & Social Change, 74*, 608–626.

Phan, P., Zhou, J., & Abrahamson, E. (2010). Creativity, innovation and entrepreneurship in China. *Management and Organization Review, 6*(2), 175–194.

Ratten, V. (2012). Entrepreneurship, e-finance and mobile banking. *International Journal of Electronic Finance, 6*(1), 1–12.

Ratten, V. (2013). Cloud computing: A social cognitive perspective of ethics, entrepreneurship, technology marketing, computer self-efficacy and outcome expectancy on behavioural intentions. *Australasian Marketing Journal (AMJ), 21*(3), 137–146.

Ratten, V. (2014). Future research directions for collective entrepreneurship in developing countries: A small and medium-sized enterprise perspective. *International Journal of Entrepreneurship and Small Business, 22*(2), 266–274.

Ratten, V. (2017). Entrepreneurial universities: The role of communities, people and places. *Journal of Enterprising Communities: People and Places in the Global Economy, 11*(3), 310–315.

Ratten, V., & Dana, L.-P. (2017). Sustainable entrepreneurship, family farms and the dairy industry. *International Journal of Social Ecology and Sustainable Development, 8*(3), 114–129.

Ratten, V., & Tajeddini, K. (2017). Innovativeness in family firms: An internationalization approach. *Review of International Business and Strategy, 27*(2), 217–230.

Ratten, V., Ramadani, V., Dana, L.-P., Hoy, F., & Ferreira, J. (2017). Family entrepreneurship and internationalization strategies. *Review of International Business and Strategy, 27*(2), 150–160.

Schumpeter, J. (1934). *The theory of economic development.* Cambridge: Harvard University Press.

Shinde, K. A. (2010). Entrepreneurship and indigenous entrepreneurs in religious tourism in India. *International Journal of Tourism Research, 12*, 523–535.

Game Changes in Sport: The Role of Innovation and Creativity

3.1 Introduction

Sport has unique characteristics, which impact the development of entrepreneurship (Ratten 2011a). There are differences in sport compared to other sectors due to the role institutions play, which requires a focus more on the context of sport in order to develop new theories about entrepreneurship. It is clear from the current rise in research about sports entrepreneurship that more theoretical and practical development are needed (Ratten 2011b). There are many types of sport that have similar characteristics but also distinctive features that need to be studied separately. Thus, there is a need to understand each sport context individually to see how entrepreneurship develops. This involves considering sport at the professional and amateur level in terms of entrepreneurship.

Sport entrepreneurs tend to act differently depending on their cultural and environmental setting. Thus, the challenge for sports entrepreneurship researchers is to understand the different cultural aspects particular to certain sports such as socio-demographic characteristics and institutional environment. For example, cricket and football are still played mostly in certain geographic areas so the economic and political conditions existing in these regions affect entrepreneurship. Sport can act as a facilitator to change perceptions about the kind of sport played in certain geographical locations as a way to encourage entrepreneurial endeavours.

The exploration of sport entrepreneurship in the context of different types of economies such as developed and emerging will allow for an understanding of necessity and opportunity driven business behavior. This will offer the potential to understand in general sports entrepreneurship and enable a way to increase research interest. The increased interest in studying sport might come from its importance in people's daily lives. This is due to sport having a continuously widespread impact on society both as a leisure pursuit but also as an economic activity.

Sports entrepreneurship is a way for an individuals or organizations to be innovative and risk taking in a sports context. There is a focus on the managerial process in sports entrepreneurship due to the need for proactive behavior in an organization. An important way to understand sports organizations in through their

V. Ratten, *Sport Entrepreneurship*, Management for Professionals,
https://doi.org/10.1007/978-3-319-73010-3_3

stakeholders. Research on sports entrepreneurship has been evolving at a slow rate in the past decade but is recently gaining momentum as more researchers realize the value of linking sport to entrepreneurship from a stakeholder perspective. Sport entrepreneurship is exciting due to the acknowledgement that sport has inherent entrepreneurial behaviours. The research field of sport entrepreneurship is building as a promising way to link the disparate sport and entrepreneurship literature. Diverse ways of understanding the role of entrepreneurship in sport enables the building of new theoretical frameworks by focusing on the game changing nature of sport. This enables the tailoring of creative ways to build research momentum around sport entrepreneurship. In addition, it helps to lead to more meaningful research that combines the practical applications of sport and entrepreneurship.

The eclectic field of sport entrepreneurship has developed as an innovative field building on the sport and entrepreneurship disciplines. Great progress has been made in advancing sport entrepreneurship in recent years with business theory meeting practical knowledge. The reality is that many different types of businesses in sport including small, large and private or public have entrepreneurial qualities. This has meant more interest on incorporating the contributions of entrepreneurship to sport business. The owning and operating of a sport business can incorporate entrepreneurial behavior.

The purpose of this chapter is to focus on the interface between entrepreneurship and sport, which has been under researched in the entrepreneurship discipline. The chapter aims to shed light on how entrepreneurial processes contribute to the dynamic nature of sport by stressing their game changing nature. This will complement existing research but extend it to ensure it is multi-disciplinary and engaged with industry. This discussion in this chapter will help address the legitimacy of sports entrepreneurship and launch more research interest in this area. A common thread amongst research on sport entrepreneurship supports the idea that sport can be understood through an entrepreneurial lens. This means increased emphasis on entrepreneurial leadership in sport is needed to increase our understanding about this rapidly growing research area.

3.2   Game Changes in Sport

Game changers are defined as "macro-phenomena (events, trends and developments) that change the 'game' of societal intersection (the roles, fields and players)" (Avelino et al. 2017: 3). Sport events have become more innovative with a mixture of entertainment, leisure and professional activities. More people are participating in sport events that link to a certain charity, region or lifestyle. This is evident in sports such as surfing that depend on weather conditions for the event to take place. Thus, there has been a trend towards televising more adventure sports due to the benefits of appealing to a greater audience. This development in sport has grown with real-time telecasting through the internet giving way to game changing occurrences in the sport context. There is also changes in some sports in terms of the rules with surfing introducing new policies in order to align more with traditional sports seen on television. For example, the highest ranked surfer on the tour wears a yellow vest like that occurring in other sports to differentiate themselves. Another example is on sport fields particularly for football games with large television audiences have introduced game lines so viewers can understand better the rules. Players in sport have also changed the way they interact by having more personalized clothing such as Roger Federer's own clothing line.

Avelino et al. (2017) suggests that the main types of game changes are demographic, ecological, political, social movements and socio-technological. Demographic changes such as the ageing population are meaning that older consumers are playing and consuming sport in different ways to younger consumers. This means that some slower paced sports such as yoga or lawn bowls are appealing to older sport consumers. In addition, the growth in people living in urban areas means there has been an increase in people frequenting indoors sports spaces such as gymnasiums.

Ecological changes include climate change that makes sustainability an important issue for sport organizations. This has lead to sport stadiums incorporating recycling and use of reusable material initiatives as part of their environmental initiatives. Political changes refer to the way sport is governed at the local, national and international level. These political changes have been evident in sports events such as the Olympics and World Cup Football that require international collaboration. In addition, there has been less funding from the government on welfare making economic concerns more evident in sports consumers. The global economic crisis in 2008 further fueled political changes with decreased spending on sport.

Social movements include the knowledge economy, which has increased the usage of online sports communication (Ratten 2012). Sport can now be viewed online in a real time format that has increased its global appeal. Socio-technical changes refer to the increased usage of technology particularly in terms of the internet-of-things where everything in connected (Ratten 2017). This has resulted in sports consumers being able to watch games on multiple devices and interact with teams on social media.

In order for sports entrepreneurship to succeed there needs to be a vision about how the innovation will change existing conditions. Visions should be conducted in different time periods including immediate, short and long term plans (Santos et al. 2017). This helps to predict the future by planning for change and mitigating risk. Mont et al. (2014: 31) states visions "should help to explore "hard to imagine" events and consequences and prepare a smooth transition to new societal modes". In sport the hard to imagine events include new contests and ways of playing the game. Thus, it is important to plan for the future by keeping in mind different scenarios about how business practices will change (Tajeddini and Ratten 2017). This includes re-imagining sport business models that involve experimentation with different innovations. In order to advance society, it is helpful to focus on behavioural changes that are a result of demographic shifts. Mont et al. (2014) suggests that creating a culture of innovation dialogues through long term thinking is important. This will encourage thinking about how to develop an understanding of the reasons why entrepreneurship is common in sport.

3.3   Innovation

There are different ways people can contribute to innovation including ideas, opinions, positions, suggestions and thoughts (Mascia et al. 2015). This makes innovation a dynamic and iterative process, which changes over time (Tsiotsou and Ratten 2010). There is also a complex web of information leading to innovation that is based on collaboration. Individuals collaborate to enhance innovation in sport by facilitating the ideation process(Gërguri-Rashiti et al. 2017). Sport has typically been delivered through organizations that are commercial, public or voluntary (Misener and Misener 2017). Commercial sport organizations have become larger and more international in recent years due to the global appeal of sport. The key focus in commercial sport organizations is on competitiveness in the marketplace. Thus, there is a need to be profitable in these organizations through offering distinct products or services. In order to help commercial sport organizations remain competitive they often partner with non-profit or public organizations in order to broaden their market appeal (Misener and Misener 2017). Public sector sport organizations are those offered by government entities for the benefit of society. Due to financial pressures being placed on governments there has been more emphasis on revenue generating activities in public sector sport organizations. This is due to the amount of government resources spent on sport so there needs to be a positive public perception about spending initiatives. Some public sector sport providers have partnered with other organizations in order to outsource some services. This is due to some sport services requiring more resources than the government can provide. Voluntary sport organizations operate on the basis of non-paid workers giving their time for a sport purpose. Sometimes they are referred to as nonprofit entities due to the social role they play in the sport context. Many amateur sport clubs are non-profit in nature but have a management structure similar to many corporate organizations. This has led to voluntary sport organizations changing to more hybrid structures that have both volunteers and paid employees. This helps create a more transparent and efficient organizational structure.

Innovation can be described as a democratic process involving customers, employees and other individuals suggesting ideas and providing feedback (Mascia et al. 2015). This democratic form of cooperation empowers people to contribute to the innovation process. There are different contributions individuals make to innovation particularly those that are part of large communities. This includes their experience and knowledge about sports that can help make innovation a reality. Stronger collaborative ties between individuals are likely to result in more innovation (Ahuja 2000). This provides a way of capturing creative ideas that lead to sport innovation. There are also direct and indirect ties between individuals that impact problem solving abilities in terms of the directions sport innovation may take. Network ties are important in influencing social structures around innovation but change over time (Mascia et al. 2015). In sport, these network ties occur in a variety of contexts including between players, coaches and fans.

An essential outcome for most sports organizations is the generation of entrepreneurial ideas. This is reflected in entrepreneurship contributing to the growth and survival of many sports organizations. Zacher and Rosing (2015: 54) states "innovation is the result of both individual factors (e.g. cognitive abilities, personality and motivation) and contextual factors (e.g. work characteristics and leadership". Individual factors in sport range from the ability of athletes to utilize their connections and knowledge to derive innovative ideas. These innovations may depend on the personality of the athletes in terms of their willingness to take risk. Some athletes will be motivated to be innovative for financial reasons but others for non-profit or social gain. Contextual factors involve where a sport organizations is situated. This is important as some sports organizations are located in regions that may have better entrepreneurial ecosystems. Thus, the context in which a sports organization resides helps determine its entrepreneurial behavior. There is also the role of work characteristics in that some sports organizations will encourage more innovative behavior in their workplaces. The ambidextrous theory of leadership for innovation proposes that leaders have both exploitative and exploration behaviours that facilitate innovation (Rosing et al. 2011). This helps to encourage innovative leadership that harnesses change as a form of strategic direction (Tajeddini et al. 2017).

Innovation is defined as "a process of developing, adopting, and applying new ideas to generate new products, practices, programs, policies, technologies, services or structures for organizational members" (Comeaux 2013: 284). In a sport context this means organizations need to actively engage in a process of developing ideas that can be applied in the marketplace. This requires interpreting trends to see how new ideas can progress in sport in order to derive new processes. Simmie and Strambach (2006: 28) take an evolutionary economics view of innovation by defining it as "an interactive learning system that develops through time and in which history, social and political forces all play a part in addition to purely economic factors". Thus, innovation can be described as chaos within guidelines. Schweisfurth and Herstatt (2014: 1) states "innovation happens if knowledge of market needs and technological solutions are combined". In sport some knowledge about market needs is uncertain and depends on consumer acceptance. Therefore, when technological solutions are made in a sport context it helps gain acceptance in the marketplace.

Innovation is an elusive concept with a wide range of definitions. Alonso and Bressan (2016: 311) suggests innovation includes "ideas for improving communication, reorganizing, introducing new budgeting systems or cutting costs". When new ideas are introduced into the sports marketplace they need to be accepted by consumers in order to succeed. Not all sports organizations benefit from innovation due to the costs and time associated with changes. In addition, despite the advantages of innovation there are transaction costs and relationship changes that need to be made (Bunduchi et al. 2011). Studies focusing on the role of innovation in sport are scarce, which is unusual given the amount of change from technological advances. There is a historical legacy of innovation in some particular sports that are known for their innovativeness such as surfing. Other sports are more conservative such as football so the innovation is not in the game but in the clothing.

Alves et al. (2007: 28) states "innovative organizations exploit various sources of ideas for new products and stimulate employees' imagination in order to fill the pipeline that nourishes new products". Thus in a sport setting innovation is important in progressing ideas that play a role in the organizational capacity for change. Often new ideas are conceptualized in sport but taken to other industries due to their inter-industry capacity. There are three main stages of the innovation process: fuzzy front end, new product development and commercialization (Alves et al. 2007). The first stage is the fuzzy front end, which involves the coming up with ideas that might occur in an unpredictable manner. Some ideas are relatively straightforward in terms of how they are introduced into the marketplace but others take a more unstructured path that makes them hard to predict. In the fuzzy front end stage it is normally involves more time than money as is a form of brainstorming activity. Flynn et al. (2003) suggests that it is important to try and develop as many ideas as possible at the start of the new product development process in order to influence the number that make it into the marketplace. The second stage is new product development, which involves experimenting with different approaches to find the best one that works. This involves changing ideas to suit the context and utilizing resources to make ideas a reality. Alves et al. (2007: 28) suggests that these ideas have criteria "that often escape rational analysis, being rooted in intuitive evaluations, internal and external politic considerations and opportunistic preoccupations". The third stage is about commercialization and involves developing a business plan based on projected goals. Commercialization is a more rational process as it requires project management based on financial and resource requirements.

The studying of new venture creation is important for the sport industry as it influences the long term performance of firms and the sustainability of business structures. In innovative business ventures there is generally more uncertainty with future potential, which makes it difficult to ascertain how long it will take for ideas to get into the marketplace. This gestation period means that there tends to be more resources devoted to innovation with the hope that some will pay off in the future. To make progress with these innovative business ventures there should be more focus on human capital particularly in the form of social networks that can make these ideas a reality.

Efrat et al. (2016: 3) defines innovativeness as "any operation that's different from conventional strategy in marketing or sales, for example". The key part of this definition is the acknowledgement that differences in strategy is important in staying at the forefront of the sport industry. Another definition is proposed by Craig et al. (2014) who states firm innovativeness is "a firm's willingness to place strong emphasis on technological developments, new products, new services, and/or improved product lines in pursuit of competitive advantage". This means that firm innovativeness changes the nature of competition in the sport industry. In sport firms, innovativeness can range from minor changes in processes to major improvements in the way services are conducted. Lechner and Gudmundsson (2014: 40) states that innovativeness involves "a strong R&D emphasis, technological leadership, the introduction of new products and the degree of changes in product or service lines". Depending on a firm's competitive strategy the level of innovativeness will change depending on environmental context.

Efrat et al. (2016: 3) defines an innovative product as "one that meets an existing need, a need, that already had previous solutions, but were all very different from the new one". This definition emphasizes that adapting an existing product in a new way can be innovative or alternatively there is a completely new product. Kotha et al. (2011) in a study of young and old biotechnology firms analyzed differences in innovation output. They found that the younger firms tended to have innovations associated with higher impact as measured by greater numbers of forward citations. This suggests that there is more propensity for younger firms to derive new ideas that will produce a stream of innovations. This is a form of circular economy in that the ideas foster other innovations, which contribute to a more innovative society. The older firms were found to have a higher quantity of innovation output as measured by the greater levels of filed patent applications.

In the rapidly changing sport business environment, entrepreneurship offers a way for organizations to remain competitive. Maritz and Donavan (2015: 74) states that innovation refers to "the development, adoption and exploitation of value-added activities in economic and social areas". Embracing an entrepreneurial attitude in sport organizations enables better competitiveness. Despite the practical linkage between the topics of entrepreneurship and sport, each distinct area has a separate body of knowledge. Innovation is a common theme in sport but there is a lack of research about its distinctiveness in a sport context. This could be due to the ambiguity of the word innovation in entrepreneurship research (Maritz and Donovan 2015). Innovation can be both an outcome and process that is dependent on the exploitation of novel ideas (Crossan and Apaydin 2010). In sports innovation it is used to produce new products or services that enable better performance outcomes. Thus, innovation is a tool that can be used in sport to exploit changes that are part of the entrepreneurial process. Entrepreneurship provides a way to explain the how, when, where and why of opportunities.

Innovation systems in sport help create networks of individuals and organizations that can focus on bringing new ideas into economic usage. Entrepreneurship takes on many different forms, which vary according to environmental context. Yigitcanlar and Bulu (2016: 2) states innovation spaces are "integrated centers of knowledge generation, learning and commercialization, and lifestyle experimentation". These innovation spaces are encouraged in sport as a way to combine innovation activities that bring about a change to the types of sport popular in a marketplace. Konnala et al. (2007) suggests that there are three major components to the performance of innovation systems: (1) setting scientific and technological goals, (2) connecting and efficiency and (3) shared awareness. The first stage involves setting priorities for scientific and technological goals about sport innovation systems due to the need for entities to work together on shared projects. This means using planning systems designed to measure and evaluate each set of the innovation process. Depending on the nature of the sports innovation it may require more emphasis on scientific research in order to evaluate its potential usefulness in the market. This normally applies to sports medicine as it needs a review process to ensure it meets market regulations. New sport technologies are likely to enter the market faster as they do not require as much regulatory approval.

However, the sports technology in terms of its development will be affected by the complexity of the product or service. Some sports technologies can complement existing products in the marketplace but the ones that are entirely new may need more time to be tested before reaching the final stage of development. The second stage involves connecting different members of the innovation system together so that there is a mutually beneficial exchange of information. This is important in ensuring that there is an efficient dissemination of information about tasks and what needs to be completed. The third stage is about creating an awareness in the marketplace about future technologies.

The goal of innovation is to achieve a better result, which can include increased profitability or marketshare. Some innovation can result in better prestige through a recognition of creative endeavours. The advancement of scientific knowledge can result in technological changes in sport. When an organization decides to implement an innovation there are decision costs. These costs include "management or technical skill time and costs of collecting information" (Alonso and Bressan 2016: 314). In a sport environment the decision costs depend on how quickly the innovation needs to be implemented into the marketplace. There is some instability in organizations when deciding the appropriate time to enter an innovation in the market. This is due to decision makers having uncertainty about the level of success for the innovation. There is the possibility that some sports innovations will take a while to adopt because of the lack of confidence in consumer acceptance. Decisions about how to cooperate and use resources are needed about sport innovations. Innovation is a fascinating topic in sports due to the level of variety in the way collaborative processes lead to innovation. Some of the most predominant forms of innovating involve making decisions on the adoption of equipment and new technology.

3.4   Employee Innovation

Employees play an important role in taking the first step and managing subsequent processes about innovation in organizations (Schweisfurth and Herstatt 2014). Innovation can be enhanced when employees focus on creativity as part of the development of innovation. In organizations, contextual factors such as leadership and time allocation help build innovative capacities. This is due to organizational leaders playing a crucial role in getting ideas off the ground from the initial conceptual stage. Thus, there are a number of benefits for sports organizations engaging in innovative initiatives. New knowledge can be supported in the sport industry through education policies around innovation. To enhance the prospects of the sport industries success there needs to be a focus on improving innovation.

There are also employee traits such as job descriptions and responsibilities that impact the ability of organizations to be innovative. The role of employees in sport organizations refers to people paid for performing certain tasks but there is also a lot of volunteers in a sports context. Therefore, employees of sports organizations need to utilize their knowledge about work processes to connect with volunteers who may help in the innovation process. As such, employees can transfer organizational knowledge to outside entities to develop sports innovation. The absorption of sports knowledge is a challenge for people outside organizations making it important to combine resources. A major dilemma for sports organizations is how to capitalize on employees knowledge about potential useful innovations. Foroudi et al. (2016: 4883) states that innovation is "an approach to creating an appropriate, simple and flexible business model, which can serve the interests of managers or consumers in a competitive market". This means that managers need to focus on ways to help their employees and consumers come up with innovative ideas in a sports context.

Employees can interpret potential innovations by drawing on their knowledge about organizational processes. This can foster corporate innovation that embeds employees, volunteers and users of sport in the innovation process. By embedding people in the innovation it helps to foster shared learning processes. Barnes and Mattsson (2016:96) states the innovation process includes "the search for, experimentation with and discovery, development, imitation and adaptation". Sport has loyal communities that can help with the innovation process due to their commitment to certain teams. In a sports context, many users are outside an organization, which makes it hard for them to be involved in innovation. Thus, it is helpful for employees to connect with sport users to facilitate their contribution to innovation. In order for innovation to succeed it needs to be integrated into a local ecosystem. This relies on managers facilitating innovation through information dissemination and modification. Sport managers need to exchange information and knowledge related to the innovation in order to identify new opportunities.

Schweisfurth and Herstatt (2014: 3) states "employee innovation has not only been related to the context inside the firm, but also to the extent to which employees can access resources outside the organization". This means that employees need to acquire external knowledge that can be transferred to their organization. Thereby the employees span the boundary of their organization to connect with others. The traditional management philosophy in many sports organizations was to continue to advance existing products that were profitable at the expense of funding new growth. In the entrepreneurial economy, however, there is a need to foresee trends before they occur and devote resources to new sports innovations. Thus, it is crucial for sports organizations to identify growth avenues as a way to transform the market. This means sport organizations should develop key competences that support innovation by focusing on their core competences. Sport organizations that master the entrepreneurial process will find themselves in better market positions. By understanding the relationship between entrepreneurship and growth, sports organizations can formulate better strategies. Table 3.1 states how the individual capacities of embedded sport users affect the innovation process.

Table 3.1 Individual capacities of embedded sport users within the innovation process

Phase	Individual capability	Examples
Development	Product testing Specification setting	Trailing new ideas about sport innovation Seeing if the sports innovation requires any changes
Ideation	Competitive intelligence External information absorption Idea generation	Knowing what other sports companies are doing Exchanging information with other sports enthusiasts about ideas Asking others opinions about potential sports innovation
Marketing	Company representation Opinion leadership	Becoming champion of the sports innovation Fostering communication about the benefits of the sports innovation

Adapted from Schweisfurth and Herstatt (2014)

3.5　Social Innovation

Avelino et al. (2017: 3) defines social innovation as "changing social relations, involving new ways of doing, organizing, framing and knowing". Social innovation is important in sport due to the vast array of non-profit entities and community role that sport plays in the world. A core component of social innovation is new ways of organizing sport, which is evident in the charity and fun run races that have grown in popularity. In addition, professional sport has changed with athletes and players as contributing to society through outreach activities. This helps bridge the gap between the money making aspect of sport with the charitable benefits stemming coming from a sports environment. Social innovation enables better collective empowerment as individuals group together for particular causes (Moulaert 2013). By knowing that sport teams can help encourage positive behaviours in society this leads to better perceptions of the impact of sport in communities. This is evident in football teams wearing logos from charities on their uniforms for free or spending time on volunteer activities that engage with communities. Sport is a form of social innovation when the way people behave in sport has a public benefit.

3.6　Systems Innovation

System innovation is defined as "a process of structural change at the level of societal (sub)-systems with functional and/or spatial delineations (eg health, welfare, energy, transport, city, region)" (Avelino et al. 2017: 3). In sport there are specific changes in systems that have transformed the industry. This is evident in health issues such as heart rates being measured on smart watches that athletes can wear. In addition, there has been new sports technology related to health such as training initiatives that have changed coaching processes. Cities and regions have also changed sport systems to be more competitive at the global level. This is seen in more public transport systems going to sport stadiums and arenas. Moreover, energy at sport arenas has been altered in many regions to be more efficient. This is seen in solar and wind power providing energy that saves money but is also an innovation for sport. The most important system innovations change cultural assumptions and this can include knowledge and physical infrastructure (Grin et al. 2010).

3.7 Creativity Process in Sport

New ideas are important in sport in terms of planning and forecasting change. Sometimes brainstorming is a way to derive new ideas as they enable the combination of innovation with strategic planning. Creativity tends to flow when there are new ideas coming from multidisciplinary perspectives, which is important to sport. This means that a market orientated focus is needed to sort out the best new ideas to see how they can be commercialized. For some it helps to list ideas based on their feasibility and quality. Feasibility means how much money and time they will take to develop and their likely impact on the sports market. Amateur sports organizations that come up with new ideas may need to partner with government entities or private organizations in order to help with the commercialization process. Quality is measured in terms of the product or service lifecycle and the resulting profit revenues. It is important for sport organizations to focus on the quality of new ideas so that time can be devoted to appropriate issues. New ideas after they are evaluated for feasibility and quality need to be followed up in terms of progress to ensure they survive to the next stage. This means gaining opinions from various stakeholders taking a multidisciplinary approach to ensure different points of view are considered. This can involve feedback and opinion about progress based on timetables. Some new ideas will be scheduled by their contribution to the overall performance of a sports organization. It is important to focus on new ideas once at a time to ensure they are fully developed in the sports context.

After new ideas have progressed they can then be classified based on appeal to the sport marketplace. This involves focusing on selecting the best new ideas in order to explore their likely market potential. Often decisions about new ideas are based on intuition rather than a set of rigid rules. This means that it is important to have a multidisciplinary perspective in the sports context to develop new ideas. Sometimes spontaneous choices based on feedback from sports people will help the best new ideas gain traction. Once a new idea has progressed and been developed then it needs to get the appropriate attention from marketers who can advertise its beneficial features. The decisions sports marketers make will be based on their familiarness with the new ideas but also their vision for the future. Thus, it is crucial to ensure that new ideas are advertised in the best way based on market appeal. Advertising can utilize athletes that have brand recognition and credibility in the marketplace. The attitudes of marketers to the new ideas is important in order to allow for the best campaigns. Some sports marketing will be adapted based on suggestions and changes in the way new ideas are viewed by consumers.

Johannisson (2012: 1) states "entrepreneurship and innovation have been surfacing as key words in policy and academic discourse on the ordering of the economy and competitiveness of regions". As part of this discourse is the focus on sport-related entrepreneurship and innovation, which helps influence economic and social growth. The importance of sports bodies and authorities focusing on creativity is embedded in policy documents and business partnerships. Sport is a key component of the global economy as it helps boost economies and contributes to society. One of the biggest research gaps within current entrepreneurship studies is the link with sport. This has meant that there are research issues to address around sport entrepreneurship particularly in terms of how sport entities utilize entrepreneurship to fulfill their ambitions.

There are a number of factors that influence the creative process in sport, which are stated in Table 3.2. These factors are part of both the internal and external environment affecting sport organizations in terms of how they develop creative ideas that lead to innovation. The internal environment involves the organizational culture in terms of how decisions are made and information disseminated. More innovative organizations tend to have an innovation culture that stresses the role of creativity in the ideation process and the need for new thinking. Often innovative organizations will utilize operational objectives that relate to innovation as a way to

Table 3.2 Factors influencing the creative process in sport

Factors	Examples
Organizational strategy	Role of innovation in performance
	Shared vision about innovation
	Innovation oriented projects
Resource availability	New idea generation
	Availability of time
	Finances devoted to new processes
New technologies	High risk ventures
	Technology cooperation
	Creative problem solving
R&D intensity	Product development
	Stimulation of technologies
	Communication channels
Culture and motivation	Shared values and beliefs
	Frequency of creative occurrences
	Level of innovation
Communication	Capacity to collaborate
	Adapt to changes
	Openness
Organizational structure	Dynamic contact between departments
	Flexibility and freedom
	Empowerment in decision making
Employee involvement	Role in idea evaluation
	Quality of human resources
	Reward systems

Adapted from Alves et al. (2007)

stay competitive. Alves et al. (2007: 28) states that "the external environment for innovation within which organizations operate includes the institutional support basis and relevant sets of values and norms". Thus, the external environment impacts the rules and regulations that organizations need to consider in terms of how they develop creativity. This is important in terms of generating new ideas that can generate additional profits.

Some organizations focus on the synergies they can create based on the institutional support from governments based on policy initiatives. This is helpful in obtaining loans and grants that can support research into new processes that lead to the generation of innovation. In sport organizations there is a need to consider also the values they have in terms of connection with the community and social benefits of sport. This means that there are some relational norms in terms of codes of conduct and behavior that influence the way creativity is developed in an organization in response to external stimuli.

3.8 Networks

Networks in a sport context often involve social interaction that facilitates the flow of information. These social networks play an important role in facilitating the construction of new ideas. Some networks foster collaboration between people within organizations as a way of sharing knowledge leading to innovation. The importance of networks has been made more evident by technology changes necessitating fast thinking. Thus, networks are a way firms can achieve better competitive advantage in their marketplace through observing what others are doing as a response to change. There needs to be a linkage between the use of networks and strategies that organizations develop. Entrepreneurship has paved the way for more sport organizations to use their networks. The success of entrepreneurial endeavours in sport requires an intimate link with social networks. This is due to social networks facilitating the use of innovative capabilities that lead to sports entrepreneurship. The capacity of sports organizations to generate innovation is based on their entrepreneurial orientation.

Networks in sport help enhance creative processes by sharing knowledge. This is due to the combination of different types of people and organizations working together to provide a fertile ground for creativity to develop. People in sport have distinct mindsets, which are partly influenced by the type of organization they work in and their prior experience. Some people are more entrepreneurial due to their position within an organization but also personal traits towards risk and innovation. This means that there will be different types of interests people have that can make networks are useful way to disseminate information. In networks it helps to have diversity as it paves the way for new products and ideas to develop. This is useful in bringing together multidisciplinary sport products that need input from different areas. For example, new sports nutrition products are developed by sports medicine authorities in partnership with athletes. This makes the products more complex but also innovative in their usages.

3.9   Conclusion

This chapter has looked at the role of creativity in developing entrepreneurship in sport. This is a research area that is still progressing but is linked to the creativity, innovation and sport context. There is a complementarity nature between sport and entrepreneurship that plays an important role in producing more ideas that can be commercialized. Thus, there is a need in sport to focus on intuition but also use rational methods to assess viable entrepreneurial business ventures. Due to the vast array of different stakeholders in sport there is a need to utilize diverse skills in order to develop entrepreneurship. This contributes to better entrepreneurship in sport that utilizes problem solving and network capacity as a way to grow ideas.

References

Ahuja, G. (2000). Collaboration networks, structural holes and innovation: A longitudinal study. *Administrative Science Quarterly, 45*, 425–455.

Alonso, A. D., & Bressan, A. (2016). Micro and small business innovation in a traditional industry. *International Journal of Innovation Science, 8*(4), 311–330.

Alves, J., Marques, M. J., Saur, I., & Marques, P. (2007). Creativity and innovation through multidisciplinary and multisectoral cooperation. *Creativity and Innovation Management, 16* (1), 27–34.

Avelino, F., Wittmayer, J. M., Pel, B., Weaver, P., Dumitru, A., Haxeltine, A., Kemp, R., Jorgensen, M. S., Bauler, T., Ruijsink, S., & O'Riordan, T. (2017) Transformative social innovation and (dis) empowerment. *Technological Forecasting & Social Change,* Available online 7 June 2017, https://doi.org/10.1016/j.techfore.2017.05.002

Barnes, S. J., & Mattsson, J. (2016). Building tribal communities in the collaborative economy: An innovation framework. *Prometheus, 34*(2), 95–113.

Bunduchi, R., Weisshaar, C., & Smart, A. U. (2011). Mapping the benefits and costs associated with process innovation: The case of RFID adoption. *Technovation, 31*(9), 505–521.

Comeaux, E. (2013). Rethinking academic reform and encouraging organizational innovation: Implications for stakeholder management in college sports. *Innovation Higher Education, 38,* 281–293.

Craig, J. B., Dibrell, C., & Garrett, R. (2014). Examining relationships among family influence, family culture, flexible planning systems, innovativeness and firm performance. *Journal of Family Business Strategy, 5*, 229–238.

Crossan, M. M., & Apaydin, M. (2010). A multi-dimensional framework of organizational innovation: A systematic review of the literature. *Journal of Management Studies, 47*(6), 1154–1191.

Efrat, K., Gilboa, S., & Yonatany, M. (2017). When marketing and innovation interact: The case of born-global firms.International Business Review, 26(2), 380-390.

Flynn, M., Dooley, L., O'Sullivan, D., & Cormican, K. (2003). Idea management for organizational innovation. *International Journal of Innovation Management, 7*, 417–442.

Foroudi, P., Jin, Z., Gupta, S., Melewar, T. C., & Foroudi, M. M. (2016). Influence of innovation capability and customer experience on reputation and loyalty. *Journal of Business Research, 69*, 4882–4889.

Gërguri-Rashiti, S., Ramadani, V., Abazi-Alili, H., Dana, L.-P., & Ratten, V. (2017). ICT, innovation and firm performance: The transition economies context. *Thunderbird International Business Review, 59*(1), 93–102.

Grin, J., Rotmans, J., & Schot, J. (2010). *Transitions to sustainable development: New directions in the study of long term transformative change.* New York: Routledge.

Johannisson, B. (2012). Entrepreneurship: The practice of cunning intelligence. In *Swedish Entrepreneurship Forum: 20 years of entrepreneurship research* (pp. 109–119).

Konnala, T., Brummer, V., & Salo, A. (2007). Diversity in foresight: Insights from the fostering of innovation ideas. *Technological Forecasting and Social Change, 74*(5), 608–626.

Kotha, R., Zheng, Y., & George, G. (2011). Entry into new niches: The effects of firm age and the expansion of technological capabilities on innovative output and impact. *Strategic Management Journal, 32*(9), 1011–1024.

Lechner, C., & Gudmundsson, S. V. (2014). Entrepreneurial orientation, firm strategy and small firm performance. *International Small Business Journal, 32*(1), 36–60.

Mascia, D., Magnusson, M., & Bjork, J. (2015). The role of social networks in organizing ideation, creation and innovation: An introduction. *Creativity and Innovation Management, 24*(1), 102–107.

Maritz, A., & Donovan, J. (2015). Entrepreneurship and innovation: Setting an agenda for greater discipline contextualisation. *Education+ Training, 57*(1), 74–87.

Misener, K. E., & Misener, L. (2017). Grey is the new black: Advancing understanding of new organizational forms and blurring sector boundaries in sport management. *Journal of Sport Management, 31*, 125–132.

Mont, O., Neuvonen, A., & Lahteenoja, S. (2014). Sustainable lifestyles 2050: Stakeholder visions, emerging practices and future research. *Journal of Cleaner Production, 63*, 24–32.

Moulaert, F. (2013). *The international handbook on social innovation collective action, social learning and transdisciplinary research*. Cheltenham: Edward Elgar.

Ratten, V. (2011a). A social perspective of sports-based entrepreneurship. *International Journal of Entrepreneurship and Small Business, 12*(3), 314–326.

Ratten, V. (2011b). Practical implications and future research directions for international sports management. *Thunderbird International Business Review, 53*(6), 763–770.

Ratten, V. (2012). Entrepreneurial and ethical adoption behaviour of cloud computing. *The Journal of High Technology Management Research, 23*(2), 155–164.

Ratten, V. (2017). Gender entrepreneurship and global marketing. *Journal of Global Marketing, 30*(3), 114–121.

Rosing, K., Frese, M., & Bausch, A. (2011). Explaining the heterogeneity of the leadership-innovation relationship: Ambidextrous leadership. *Leadership Quarterly, 22*(5), 956–974.

Santos, G., Marques, C., Ferreira, J., Gerry, C., & Ratten, V. (2017). Women's entrepreneurship in Northern Portugal: Psychological factors versus contextual influences in the economic downturn. *World Review of Entrepreneurship, Management and Sustainable Development, 13*(4), 418–440.

Schweisfurth, T. G., & Herstatt, C. (2014). How internal users contribute to corporate product innovation: The case of embedded users. *R&D Management, 46*, 107–126.

Simmie, J., & Strambach, S. (2006). The contribution of KIBS to innovation in cities: An evolutionary and institutional perspective. *Journal of Knowledge Management, 10*(5), 26–40.

Tajeddini, K., & Ratten, V. (2017). The moderating effect of brand orientation on inter-firm market orientation and performance. *Journal of Strategic Marketing*, Available online 21 February 2017, https://doi.org/10.1080/0965254X.2017.1293138.

Tajeddini, K., Altinay, L., & Ratten, V. (2017). Service innovativeness and the structuring of organizations: The moderating roles of learning orientation and inter-functional coordination. *International Journal of Hospitality Management, 65*, 100–114.

Tsiotsou, R., & Ratten, V. (2010). Future research directions in tourism marketing. *Marketing Intelligence & Planning, 28*(4), 533–544.

Yigitcanlar, T., & Bulu, M. (2016). Urban knowledge and innovation spaces. *Journal of Urban Technology, 23*(1), 1–9.

Zacher, H., & Rosing, K. (2015). Ambidextrous leadership and team innovation. *Leadership & Organization Development Journal, 36*(1), 5.

Athlete Entrepreneurs

4

4.1 Introduction

In this chapter, I propose that more research about athlete entrepreneurship is needed (a) to develop a better theoretical framework and (b) to promote new research and practitioner interest in this topic. Thus, athlete entrepreneurship can lead to more positive gains in learning about how entrepreneurship occurs in a sports context. This is important as athletes in sport need to forge more entrepreneurial behaviours to address the market realities. The future success of the sports industry will depend on the ability of athletes to incorporate entrepreneurship.

Athletes from a young age and in all types of sport are receiving more advice about business. This is due to the natural link between sport and business. Often sport teams are at the centre of communities and this impacts their ability to engage in business ventures. Some athletes are considered good leaders and this impacts their way they link in with other stakeholders of their community. The associations made on the sports filed become useful when an athlete finishes their playing career. Often athletes have not had the time to develop other interests so rely on their social capital when the time comes to find another career. People in the community who know the athlete from their sporting pursuits will sometimes associate the social aspects with business needs.

Athletes have been entrepreneurial in fashion by wearing new styles of clothing. This is evident in tennis as in the past most clothing was white then changed to have a specific colour for each season. Fluroscent clothing or different shades of colour have meant that tennis clothing is a fashion item. In addition, the wearing of one piece dresses in tennis was initially innovative but gained acceptance. Despite the use of different colours in tennis clothes some events such as Wimbledon still require the wearing of white clothing. There is also fashion associated with hair styles in sport that have become more evident in recent years. In football, men's hair is particularly has been a way to show individuality and self expression. Tattoos are also the norm amongst football players and considered as a fashion accessory. In addition, the length of football shorts has changed based on the evolution of fashion. Football shoes were once mostly black but have also become

© Springer International Publishing AG 2018
V. Ratten, *Sport Entrepreneurship*, Management for Professionals,
https://doi.org/10.1007/978-3-319-73010-3_4

fashion items that change in colour. Sports clothing has also been worn in more non-sporting settings than in the past. More people are wearing sportswear as leisurewear due to its comfortable and fashionable nature. This has meant that sport is increasingly seen as a forum for new fashion to develop.

The goal of this chapter is to develop a better understanding of athlete entrepreneurship. This will help many organizations to be guided by the most important factors affecting the development of athlete entrepreneurship in a sport context. A discussion of the various facets of athlete entrepreneurship is conducted to understand the diversity of the entrepreneurship process. This helps to analyse the contribution of athlete entrepreneurship to sport and its impact on society.

4.2   Athlete Entrepreneurship

Athletes are often entrepreneurial in the way they develop new products and services related to sport. As competition is at the heart of sport, athletes both amateur and professional develop new processes as part of their position within the sport ecosystem. Sometimes the innovation occurs in terms of the way the game is played as new technology is introduced into the marketplace, which changes the competitive dynamics. This means that sport needs to adopt to the new technology and this can involve a change in playing procedures or athlete attire. Due to innovations in broadcast media and the internet there has been an evolution in sport being communicated in real time. This has changed the way athletes converse with fans as there has been the introduction of social media and related internet applications.

For most sports the use of social media during an actual game is not permitted by an athlete's coach. However, fans and supporters can use social media during sport games. This has meant a more interactive experience within a game as social media enables more communication without regard to geographic location. During sports events there is social media from coaches, organizers, spectators and advertisers as they attempt to create buzz about a game. This has led to athletes being savvier about social media as a way to connect more with fans but also build their brand image. Some athletes go beyond the confines of the game to post pictures on social media showing a different side to their personality. This has meant that some athletes such as Alana Blanchard the female surfer have the most followers on Instagram and more than the male surfers due to their lifestyle posts. Alana Blanchard despite not being ranked as the world number one in women's surfing has attracted sponsorship and media attention due to her Instagram postings. Other surfers have decided not to follow the same route by focusing more on the game. This has resulted in some criticism of the way athletes use social media to promote themselves. In addition, the social media websites now available to athletes are constantly changing so they need to keep up to date with trends. This means athletes can be entrepreneurial with the way they engage with new technology.

Facebook when it first entered the market was considered innovative but then became more of a standard way to engage with people in social media. Now

Facebook is considered archaic and new forms of social media have emerged such as Twitter. Athletes themselves particularly those in team sports are known for their reliance on groups of people in their sport so it is natural for them to utilize social media as an extension of their brand. Other members of sports teams such as personal trainers also use social media as a way to gain more attention and communicate their knowledge to others. No longer is sport a separate entity to other social forms of technological communication but plays an integrated mechanism in the knowledge economy.

Some athletes are notable for their entrepreneurial spirit and business ventures. This is evident with athletes such as Greg Norman, the golf player who developed clothing, restaurants and golf courses after finishing his professional career. Other athletes have followed similar entrepreneurial routes including Michael Phelps with his own products. Thus, the reputation of an athlete on the playing field is linked to external ventures they are involved with in the business world. Due to the natural competitive personality of some athletes who have had a successful sporting career this links with their business acumen.

Athletes can educate and train themselves in a new business field or stay with the sports environment. More sports teams are seeing the need to link education with sport by supporting athletes to study. The gaining of a business or management degree is becoming more common for athletes wanting to progress in their respective sports field. Many athletes want to learn business skills that they can apply in a practical setting. In particularly, the knowledge of how to develop business plans is a useful way for athletes to progress their career. In the United States, due to age restrictions in terms of entering some professional sports leagues there is a need for athletes to gain some university education as part of being involved in collegiate sports. This has made collegiate sports in the United States popular and featuring many emerging athletes. Due to Title IX rules about equal funding for universities between male and female sports there is funding for a variety of sports. However, the male dominated sport of football is normally the most watched collegiate sport. This has resulted in football coaches being often paid more than university staff due to the popularity of the sport.

Some sports companies have started due to the founder being a previous athlete or involved in sport. This is evident with Nike, Under Armour and Adidas. There are also some new sports organizations such as Lululemon the yogawear company that begun due to the founder perceiving a gap in the market. Lululemon is perceived as a lifestyle sport brand but grew quickly as the more mainstream sport clothing companies had dismissed the potential of yogawear. Other sportswear companies such as 2XU, which is an Australian company grew from athletes seeing the need for a new type of sportswear compression tights in the marketplace. This has resulted in sports companies that are the first mover in their respective market gaining brand notoriety. Similar to other industries though such as technology the incumbent companies with the new ideas often find it hard to stay competitive when the larger more established companies enter the market. This has resulted in much acquisition and strategic alliances between the new and established sports companies. Often athletes due to their credibility in the marketplace establish new businesses as they have the social connections needed to enter the market. This makes it easier for teams to buy their goods or services due to the level of trust existing between the parties.

Collegiate athletes are amateur but often are major drawcards of their games. There is some controversy and debate about the amateur status of collegiate athletes due to the money they bring in for universities. In addition, some of these collegiate athletes do not become as popular in professional sports so miss their timeframe for revenue generating activity. The collegiate athlete system in the United States is unique and does not operate in the same way in other countries. There is sport played at universities in other countries but is not as popular as collegiate sport in the United States.

4.3   Sport Media

Sport is broadcast through a number of mediums including the internet, radio and television. This has impacted the globalization of sport as more people are able to watch or listen to sport. Increasingly there has been the use of new technology to broadcast sport such as drone technology that enables people to see sport in different ways. Previously in sports such as surfing it was hard to capture surfers but the use of drones has enabled better visibility. There is also the use of pay per view television for specific sport events such as boxing that are watched by people around the world. Television has helped internationalize sport and enabled new businesses to develop based on technological innovations. In addition, there has been an increase in the broadcasting of live sport events on television. Roberts (2017) highlights that sport is different to concerts and films when seen in a live broadcast due to its emotional characteristics with the audience. There is also competition amongst sport for viewership on television but some sports such as archery are not telegenic (Roberts 2017).

New technology has influenced sports science and engineering by enabling the use of wearable technology to monitor performance. In addition, new fabrics and equipment have affected how athletes play sport. This is evident in lightweight material in sports equipment and clothing that have revolutionized the game for athletes. Some new technology such as full body swimsuits have been banned due to their effect on swimmers performances.

New media is affecting sports as it includes interactive feedback with digital devices that encourage better participation amongst athletes. Sport has integrated new media though websites, games and blogs that encourage a more innovative way to watch and participate. More people are commenting on sport and this has affected the advertising and marketing associated with events. In addition, virtual reality is a new form of technology that has been integrated into sport. This has meant that instead of physically travelling to places people can use virtual reality to play sports. There have also been participant communities around sport that utilize websites and statistics to share information about players and teams. More freely accessible and editable websites have emerged that enable people to comment on sport. This is useful in including more media about sport that helps to build a sense of involvement in sport. Virtual communities around sport have emerged that enable more discourse but also commerce. This has created a degree of buzz about sport in terms of new approaches and player statistics.

Sports' marketing has become more entrepreneurial in terms of how promotional activities are conducted through events. This has meant that a more mass media communication strategy has been adopted for sports marketing that include digital platforms as well as traditional advertising mediums. Sports can be marketed in a number of ways including through associations, events and to the public. Typically large sport associations such as the National Basketball League have marketed sport as a form of entertainment but also through the competitive spirit of teams. This has enabled the sport to grow as teams compete for the championships. Sport events have become popular ways to market sport as they enable people to participate in the competition as athletes or spectators. These sport events are staged as ways to encourage more people to watch teams or individuals play sport. Governments have promoted sport as way to be more health and also increase the social fabric within communities.

4.4 Entrepreneurship and Athletes

Entrepreneurship is a difficult concept to define as it has different connotations depending on the personal beliefs and environmental context. Some people associate entrepreneurship with positive developments in terms of creating new businesses or ideas. However, some see it as detrimental as it involves risk and can involve financial setbacks depending on the level of economic activity. This has led to the environmental context in which entrepreneurship develops and is an important way to understand its process. Entrepreneurship has two main features: a process and capacity for change. The process of change involves doing something innovative that has not been done before as a way to progress thinking and challenge the status quo. For society to develop there needs to be processes developed that can provide new opportunities. This can be socially or economically related depending on the circumstance of the athletes involved in the entrepreneurial process. The capacity to change means that there needs to be some leadership in terms of having the capacity to organize resources for athletes. This is important in facilitating change that can have a successful outcome when managed in the right way. Both the process and capacity for change require some interaction with key stakeholders that enable the entrepreneurship to develop. This can include interaction with government officials in terms of regulating the business or local authorities in terms of managing the business venture. Most forms of athlete entrepreneurship rely on the interaction with government as part of the process in building a successful product or service.

Athlete entrepreneurs are skilful individuals that are focused on incorporating innovation into sport ventures. Most have specific personality traits that make them entrepreneurial such as being competitive and a desire to achieve. In a sport context, entrepreneurs work to build capacity around specific ideas. This helps to embed entrepreneurship within the sport context as a necessity for the longevity of the industry. Some athlete entrepreneurs are interested in their lifestyles and pursue business ventures around certain themes that fit with their own ideologies. This helps provide a motive for innovation that is in line with personal goals.

Entrepreneurship for athletes develops from the relationships between groups of people within the environment sharing a common interest. This often centers around a specific sport that requires community involvement in order to progress its development. The way entrepreneurship is used in a sports context depends on how it was designed and invented. Some entrepreneurship is calculated and developed based on specific goals and timeframes. Other forms of entrepreneurship require a degree of spontaneity in order to gain traction in the marketplace. This means that some athlete entrepreneurship will occur serendipitously depending on the cultural and market environment. Some sport cultures foster innovation as a way of gaining competitive advantage in their industries and encourage creativity. This is evident in less formal sports such as surfing where there is an artistic component to scoring, which is not evident in more formal sports. Once ideas have progressed in the sports context it requires a degree of strategy in order for them to develop in the marketplace. Networking and interaction between sports enthusiasts helps develop the innovation and foster more commercialization. However, there usually needs to be a visionary who devotes time and attention to progressing the idea beyond the initial conceptualization stage.

There are compelling benefits for encouraging athlete entrepreneurship in sport. This is due to entrepreneurship placing an emphasis on innovation and futuristic thinking that ensures change and the progression of the sport industry. This holds sports authorities more accountable for the success of entrepreneurial ideas. As such, more sport organizations have focused on entrepreneurship as a way to gain a competitive edge and allocate more specialized resources to innovation.

Sport organizations would benefit from more entrepreneurship that includes innovative approaches that promote forward thinking initiatives. Many sport organizations in their current form used performance as the primary indicator of success but this measure is ambiguous and neglects the fact that entrepreneurship can take some time to develop. Linking athletes to entrepreneurship in sport to a more comprehensive and holistic approach in an organization might contribute to better performance. This will benefit athletes in both their business and social world as it creates an environment that influences entrepreneurship. Moreover, the quality of entrepreneurial experiences for athletes needs to be better developed. This will influence the learning environment that facilitates entrepreneurship in sport. What sport organizations can do better than other industries is to encourage the sharing of ideas. This sparks creativity in a sports context and the imagination of what sport can do in society. The first step in encouraging athlete entrepreneurship is to look at the future potential of changes. However, athlete entrepreneurship goes beyond the sport industry as it affects other sectors of the economy. It is critical that sport organizations continue to focus on athlete entrepreneurship, and this need is evident in the success of new product development. The broader community benefits from athlete entrepreneurship in sport as it enables new growth and fosters innovative activity.

Currently there is a lack of research about athletes in sports entrepreneurship that must be addressed. One of the most visible ways entrepreneurship in apparent in sport has been new product development. Under the process of creating new products and services, each athlete focuses on their competitiveness. This enables growth to be maintained as a way of staying innovative. Athletes that fail to be entrepreneurial are subject to market failure in terms of loss of revenue. Once athlete entrepreneurship has been enacted in sport organizations this can strengthen their economic development. Most sport organizations that focus on athlete entrepreneurship have growth trajectories that lead to superior performance. More systemic change related to athlete entrepreneurship is required in sport.

4.5   Sport Practitioners and Entrepreneurship

Sport practitioners must manage ways to be entrepreneurial as a way to engage with new business practices. One potentially viable approach is through harnessing the entrepreneurial ecosystems that exist in the sports community. Almost all commercial sports organizations engage in entrepreneurship during the past decade. This is due to the increased realization of the market that entrepreneurial management in needed in sport activities. The goal of entrepreneurial management in sport is primarily around revenue generation. This is due to entrepreneurial skills being necessary for business growth and success.

Considerable public interest is placed on entrepreneurship in sport in order for increased commercialization and market potential. There is more priorities being placed on sport entrepreneurship due to the active engagement of the business and social roles of sport in the marketplace. Sport organizations have reformed the way they can be entrepreneurial by focusing on innovation. More sport organizations are including a plan about entrepreneurship as a way to engage in innovative outcomes. However, the question remains in a sport context, then, of how to best utilize entrepreneurial thinking. In other words, how can sport organizations bring entrepreneurship to their business practices?

During the past decade, entrepreneurship has received considerable interest in the business management literature. This is due to the realization that entrepreneurship is needed for survival in the global business world. To date, few studies about entrepreneurship have focused on sport or offered new ideas about innovations. Sport combined with entrepreneurship should be of interest to practitioners who manage organizations. This is evident with Smith and Humphries (2017: 24) stating that sport organizations are "unique cultural institutions possessing special features where standard business practices are undesirable". Thus, athletes are part of sport organizations and contribute to fostering an entrepreneurial business environment.

Sport organizations are cultural institutions as they link with culture and heritage (Smith and Humphries 2017). Most sport organizations have emotional connections that have social relevance in society. This is due to the historical significance sport has in society. Smith and Humphries (2017: 24) states "sports organizations can be seen as generic business enterprises subject to regulation, market pressure and customer demand". This means that sport organizations have a commercial role in society that requires the focus of managers.

Entrepreneurship is of interest to sport managers due to the focus on innovation and forward thinking. Sport entrepreneurship encompasses the need for creativity, development of new ideas and finding alternative revenue. The wide array of entrepreneurship in sport means that managers must pay close attention to performance implications. This can be conducted through both non-financial and financial performance evaluation techniques that take into account a more holistic understanding of sports entrepreneurship.

Roth et al. (2017: 3) states that organizations often "integrate both external and internal partners in innovation processes to achieve access to heterogenous ideas and knowledge". External partners in sport include government organizations and community groups that are interested in the progress of specific sports. Internal partners include various organizational departments such as finance and marketing that can help progress an innovation in sport.

The context in which sport is experienced has fundamentally changed over the past decade. This has been the result of information technology changes that have altered the way consumers, business and the community view sport. New technology are leading to shifts in the sport industry. The most important sports technology changes have been seen in cloud computing, data analytics management, internet of things, mobile technology, social network technology and wireless communication. These technologies have changed the way sport is personalized to consumers enabling more individualized context. In addition, there has been a deepening of connection between consumers and sport entities in terms of communication. This has led to intense interest in sports technology in terms of future opportunities and the giving of higher quality services. Therefore, sports organizations are looking to harness new technologies as a way to establish a competitive advantage in the marketplace. As a result, there has been a greater need for research about sports entrepreneurship. Optimizing entrepreneurship in sport is particularly crucial for advancing research.

Entrepreneurship has become an increasingly popular way for sports organizations to compete in the global marketplace. Yet little is known about the process of entrepreneurship in sport. In the case of sports entrepreneurship, an especially important association is the innovations and technological advancements within the industry. Thus, there are key challenges for sports entrepreneurship and ways the field can move forward in terms of encouraging more interdisciplinary research. Increased interest on sports entrepreneurship is coming from practitioners. More managers of sports organizations are seeing the need for entrepreneurship and developing practices centered on this theme. There is substantial opportunity to engage with industry using sports entrepreneurship.

There has been increased numbers of people completing fitness and health courses. However, there needs to be more educational programs about how to facilitate entrepreneurship in sport. This can include the teaching of how to run a sports enterprise such as writing a business plan, getting finance to managing employees. The educational opportunities in sports organizations need to focus on entrepreneurship as a way to facilitate creativity. In addition, there are opportunities that stem from the sport arena. Opportunities can be economic or social in nature in terms of their potential effects on the sport industry. Technology change affects the way people perceive opportunities in sport. Some opportunities are more contextualized based on current demands whilst others are focused on future events. In order to make opportunities a reality there needs to be consideration of time, resources and their implication to the sport industry. Often opportunities need to be refined and reevaluated depending on consumer perception of their usefulness. In addition, some opportunities need to be experimented with in the marketplace to assess their potential suitability.

The major advantages of sports entrepreneurship is that it brings new advances to the sport industry. This enables sport to progress and realign with market need. Sometimes ideas need to be explored based on market needs and applicability to sport. Athlete entrepreneurs utilize resources to create innovative solutions that provide newness to the sport industry. This provides them with a way to foster creativity in sport that has not been seen before.

Often athlete entrepreneurs will utilize first-hand knowledge in order to come up with innovative ideas. This is why many athlete entrepreneurs work or have previously worked in the industry. Due to social network connections it can make it easier for athlete entrepreneurs with prior market experience to gain a foothold in the industry. As technology changes at a fast rate many innovations occur when there is a linkage between market need and available finance. This requires athlete entrepreneurs to devote more time to assessing the right opportunities that fit market needs. Many athlete entrepreneurs are motivated by money but there are also some with a civic aim that want to contribute to the broader sports community.

4.6   Features of Athlete Entrepreneurship

The special features of athlete entrepreneurship that distinguish it from other types of entrepreneurship are its focus on the leisure and health sector. This requires a concentration on both public and private entities that are involved in sport. To be considered an athlete entrepreneur there needs to be an interaction with business, competition and innovation. This is due to athlete entrepreneurship making available new ideas to those who need them. In order to progress athlete entrepreneurship there needs to be communication amongst stakeholders to ensure the idea is developed. As sport often involves government bodies, it is useful to keep them involved in the process of athlete entrepreneurship. The success of sports entrepreneurship will depend on the communication between government bodies, private entities and sports enthusiasts. This means that the resulting product, service or process from the sports entrepreneurship should be communicated in an adequate way. As athlete entrepreneurship gains momentum it is then reviewed as to its progress and modifications made. Communication about the athlete entrepreneurship is part of this development in order to ensure feedback is received about potential change. In the sports context, communication can be oral in terms of market updates, television news or through social networks. Alternatively it can be in written form such as articles and reports.

4.7   Copreneurship

Copreneurs normally refer to male and females sharing involvement in a business but the collaboration can be extended to other types of partners including friends, businesses and government entities. Deacon et al. (2014: 318) states that copreneurs share "ownership, commitment and responsibility for a business". In sport, there are a variety of copreneurs due to the inclusion of both economic and social entities in the industry. This means that sometimes in sport coperneeurs have tension between the profit and non-profit motives of their business. Most sport copreneurs focus on how they can develop businesses that share in rewards based on mutual commitment. This means that sport copreneurs share labour inputs as a way of investing in the development of new businesses. Many sport businesses particularly small ones are managed by copreneurs that depending on success change to different types of management structure. Copreneurial businesses can be considered in terms of their economic, emotional, social and technical objectives (Deacon et al. 2014). In the initial stage of a sports copreneurial business there is an emphasis on the economic requirements in terms of funding. As the copreneurial business progresses the emotional aspects in terms of collaboration and working together become more important. Support from family and friends is a key part of the emotional aspects of copreneurship. This progresses into the social stage as people within the sport sector become better acquainted with the copreneurial business. Social effects of copreneurship involve asking and seeking opinions from others in the sport industry about potential business ideas. In the last stage the technical attributes of the copreneurial business become important and this includes new sports technology. Table 4.1 depicts the themes, sub-themes and how they are defined in the process of copreneurship.

Copreneurship has been an integral part of sports development from ancient to modern times. This is due to entrepreneurship enabling sport to transition from being centred around amateur offerings to being more professional in nature. Entrepreneurship is a common approach utilized by all types of sport as a way to solve problems but also progress ideas. This enables new approaches in sport to advance breaking away from the status quo. Sometimes it has been hard in sport to introduce innovative forms of behavior due to entrenched practices. This is seen in the stable forms of play and use of equipment in sport. For example, in golf there has been the required sue of balls to be a certain shape and size thereby discouraging innovation. This disincentive to innovate is also evident in sports such as football, which has had the same structured playing field that has largely remained unchanged.

Copreneurship is a way to break away from traditions in sport so that changes can be made. As the fanbase of some sports have decreased there is a realization that new

Table 4.1 Process of copreneurship

Theme	Sub-theme	Defined by
Copreneurial capacities	Human capital Social capital Cognitive social capital	Contacts, experience, knowledge Networks, trust, understanding Shared meaning, reciprocity, solidarity
Value	Economic Emotional Social Technical	Financial resources, profit Intimacy, tacit understanding Competencies, partnerships Process advancements
Sport identities	Context Self identity	Environment, industry, location Personal connection, family involvement
Process of copreneurship	Division of labour Entrepreneurial identity Reasons for involvement	Work roles and responsibilities Commitment, leadership Motivations, personal choices

Adapted from Deacon et al. (2014)

ways of doing things is needed. This is because the survival of some sports require people to realize that cultural changes are a necessity. As such, entrepreneurship has a big effect on sport in terms of introducing new sports but also maintaining and growing existing sports. In the sport industry, there needs to be a culture of fostering entrepreneurship. This entrepreneurial culture ensures that sport organizations and people reach their potential. Policies that promote enlightened ways of doing business need to be promulgated. Sports that have a pro-entrepreneurial culture can progress at a faster rate and nurture more ideas.

4.8   The Role of Sport Managers

Sport managers face a dilemma in maintaining their performance but seeking new opportunities. This means sport managers face increasing competitive pressures from other organizations trying to enter the market. There are many different factors, which led to athlete entrepreneurship in sport. For example, the emergence of new sports is a critical way of expanding into different demographic and geographical segments. An organizations creative capacity is one of the first steps in entrepreneurship. Sports entrepreneurship is a function of individual, industry and organizational systems that merge to form creative capabilities. Thus, athlete entrepreneurship is a process that involves introducing meaningful ideas that are novel to existing entities. There is a thought process of entrepreneurship as it involves the acquisition and dissemination of novel ideas.

Therefore, for athletes it is not enough just to expect entrepreneurship but it needs to be embedded within corporate culture. Management practices need to focus on how to enhance entrepreneurship and emphasise the productive use of resources. There can be a higher level of entrepreneurship in sport when there are regular efforts made at encouraging entrepreneurship. Sports managers need to formalize innovation and creativity as part of work life in order to improve entrepreneurship output.

4.9   Conclusion

This chapter progressed the literature about sport entrepreneurship by suggesting athlete entrepreneurs as a separate category. The development of athlete entrepreneurs was stated as a way of understanding the business ecosystems that develop from sport. Examples of famous athlete entrepreneurs and their business ventures was discussed as part of the inherent competitive complexity of sport. This enables the field of athlete entrepreneurship to develop and gain credibility. In summary, this chapter has taken the point of view that entrepreneurship is a necessity in sport. There is some flexibility for sports entrepreneurship research due to the fruitful areas still yet to be explored. Following my earlier discussion about the contributions of entrepreneurship to sport, there is still much to be discovered about athlete entrepreneurship. The rapid rate of technological change in sport creates a need to be more entrepreneurial. Given the practical and managerial relevance of sports entrepreneurship there are many new areas of research needed. I hope that this chapter will stimulate further interest into the way athletes influence sport entrepreneurship.

References

Deacon, I. H., Harris, J. A., & Worth, L. (2014). Who leads? Fresh insights into roles and responsibilities in a heterosexual copreneurial business. *International Journal of Gender and Entrepreneurship, 6*(3), 317–335.

Roberts, K. (2017). Sport in Europe's era of austerity: Crisis or adaptation? *International Journal of Sociology and Social Policy, 37*(1/2), 123–130.

Roth, A., Dumbach, M., Schliffka, B., & Moslein, K. (2017). Successful management of diverse corporate innovation communities. *Journal of Strategy and Management, 10*(1), 2–10.

Smith, A. C. T., & Humphries, C. (2017). A post-social conceptual framework for exploring object narratives in sport organisations. *Sport Management Review, 20*, 20–32.

Perspectives of Sport Entrepreneurship

5

5.1   Introduction

Sport has been in a flux of change based on changing market conditions and emerging technological innovations. This change is part of the development of sport due to environmental factors that influence new ways of conducting physical activity. Roberts (2017: 123) states "sport has always been a change of entity. Throughout history people have played games that we recognize as sports, though not the same sports that are played today". The role of sport in society is altering due to the impact entrepreneurship has on the industry. In order to understand different perspectives of sport entrepreneurship it is important to define what the term 'sport' means in an entrepreneurial setting.

Thiel and Mayer (2009: 83) states "in the literature on sport management, there is no agreement on a general definition of the term sports management". This means that there is a lack of consensus of how to define sports management, which makes it hard to analyze its role in entrepreneurship. Some use the term in a broad way to describe the management of health and fitness activities. However, Thiel and Mayer (2009) suggest that the lack of consensus about the term sports management is due to the word management having different meanings. For example, management can involve human resources, supply chain and technology functions. Thus, in a sport context it means that management is more multidisciplinary as it encompasses different aspects. However, management usually denotes a business approach making it easier to understand in a sport environment.

A useful definition of management in sports is espoused by Thiel and Mayer (2009: 84) as "management is not about the sports manager or the person who leads and manages a sports club, but it is about the recursive process of achieving specific aims". The key attributes of management are in adapting, mentoring and maintaining a social system (Thiel and Mayer 2009). This is due to management structures being adapted to suit the environmental context. In sport, there are a combination of profit and non-profit management structures that need to be analyzed. This requires the sport management process to be defined to see how it will function in real life.

© Springer International Publishing AG 2018   63
V. Ratten, *Sport Entrepreneurship*, Management for Professionals,
https://doi.org/10.1007/978-3-319-73010-3_5

Given the unique nature of sport, this chapter is designed to understand the entrepreneurial perspectives. Sport-based entrepreneurship theory is emerging as a good way to bridge theory and practice. This chapter presents a new area of entrepreneurship thought concerning sport. Entrepreneurship is a defining characteristic of sport and the perspectives of its application are discussed in this chapter, which is devoted to understanding entrepreneurship in sport. The purpose of this chapter is to see how entrepreneurship develops in the sport context. This chapter begins by explaining the role of lifestyle entrepreneurship in sport. The different types of sport entrepreneurship areas are then stated and major issues discussed with regards to knowledge infrastructures and leadership. The next section explains recommendations for fostering team cohesion in sport along with an agenda for having a collaborative economy. The chapter concludes by providing some implications for sport management researchers.

5.2   Sport Entrepreneurs

Sports entrepreneurs are shaping society, and in many cases more so than regulators. Often sport entrepreneurs work in collaboration with regulators to develop projects that achieve both financial and social goals. Entrepreneurship is a key requirement in sport as it drives strategic renewal and change. The development of new businesses are important factors for sustaining the role of sport in society. One of the most important messages of entrepreneurship in sport is that to be effective new ideas and processes are needed. This increases levels of sport entrepreneurship in order to facilitate innovative leadership behaviours that yield the best results.

The topic of entrepreneurship has received immense attention in the business literature but only recently in a sports context. Traditional business models in sport have changed due to the need for more sustainable and innovative products. This has led to a reinvention by sport organizations about how they deliver products and services. The main issue affecting sport organizations is how to quickly respond to market changes. This involves taking an entrepreneurship approach to explore key characteristics underpinning the growth of sports organizations.

Early research on sport business often came from a practical setting that focused on specific teams or events. Later, as sport business research evolved there was more focus on the innovation and creativity endemic in the sport industry. This linkage between sport and entrepreneurship was fueled by global attention on sporting events and companies. Entrepreneurship is a frequently mentioned word and topic in sport due to the desire to foster change. The popularity of entrepreneurship in sport is evident in the broadcasting of sports events and marketing of sport teams.

As increased pressure on sports organizations to be more self sufficient and profit orientated, managers should respond by being more entrepreneurial. Due to the early body of knowledge existing about sport entrepreneurship the discipline is still in its infancy. This provides a unique opportunity for sports entrepreneurship researchers to shape the field. Ratten (2011) was amongst the first to have a powerful impact on the development of sports entrepreneurship theory. In her groundbreaking study she proposed a sport-based theory of entrepreneurship that included a number of factors such as social, technological, environmental, economic and institutional. She suggested that sport-based entrepreneurship theory would be a new theoretical framework to link sport research and practice. This theory is being used by sport entrepreneurship researchers as a conceptual base due to its innovative premise. More sport entrepreneurship research has sprung forth realizing the vast potential of this field of study. Most of the current research is primarily focused on business but there is also an emphasis on social issues. This is due to the growing interest on sport business but has since broadened to include entrepreneurship.

Sport entrepreneurship is an interdisciplinary field with researchers hailing from a range of areas including business, engineering, finance, law and sociology. Scholars of sport entrepreneurship need to draw knowledge from a range of other disciplines and existing research. This is due to the interdisciplinary nature of sport entrepreneurship that has derived from the business, entrepreneurship and sport disciplines. Despite the considerable research on entrepreneurship there are gaps in our knowledge about how it applies to sport. In a business context, entrepreneurship typically originates as creative ideas that need to be implemented in order to create outputs. The integration of entrepreneurship research with sport management research is an underexploited area of study.

5.3   Entrepreneurship

Entrepreneurship as a discipline has grown due to the futuristic perspective towards business activity has become more important. An early definition by Knight (1921) suggested that entrepreneurship was the ability to predict the future. Recognizing that, this book focuses on the role of sport in the entrepreneurship field as a way to increase the linkage of entrepreneurship with other areas of study. Low and MacMillan (1988: 140) states "entrepreneurship is the ability to work smarter and harder than your competition". Thus, the importance of entrepreneurship to sport is reflected in its ability to encompass a range of activities. As Ireland and Webb (2007: 891) states "entrepreneurship research as a widely dispersed, loosely connected domain of issues". Entrepreneurship research is evident in many disciplines including "accounting, anthropology, economics, finance, management, marketing, operations management, political science, psychology and sociology" (Ireland and Webb 2007: 891). However, only recently has entrepreneurship been applied to a sport context.

One of the most popular theories to explain entrepreneurship is the strategic adaptation perspective. Low and MacMillan (1988: 142) states "the strategic adaptation perspective suggests that the key to entrepreneurial success lies in the decisions of the individual entrepreneur who identify opportunities, develop strategies, assemble resources and take initiatives". The strategy orientated literature in entrepreneurship focuses on how the success of a business is contingent on the development of effective strategies. This means that once a business has been started it becomes easier to evaluate information about market availability. Some business strategies are evolving based on learning from past successes and failures. This is due to much of the existing literature on entrepreneurship tending to favour the firm as the unit of analysis rather than the individual.

Nambisan (2017) suggests that there are three main perspectives in entrepreneurship research: opportunity creation, effectuation and narrative. The opportunity creation perspective involves evaluating the market then deriving appropriate actions that lead to a business being created. Opportunities about new sport producers are developed from the response of consumers and players. This includes an emphasis on the beliefs of how the product will be used in sport. The effectuation perspective involves a process of continual re-evaluation of resources and effects. Sarasvathy (2001) highlights how entrepreneurs need to engage in an iterative process in order to have a reasonable outcome. The narrative perspective suggests that entrepreneurs need to assess their environment through interaction with actors and artifacts (Nambisan 2017).

Entrepreneurship has been widely studies in business due to its impact on countries, individuals and organizations. Welter and Lasch (2008: 246) states "the entrepreneurship field will benefit from accepting wider diversity in concepts and methods". In the entrepreneurship literature there is a debate about whether opportunities are created or discovered. This stems from Audretsch et al. (2016) suggesting that the two main themes of entrepreneurship are the static and dynamic perspective. In the public domain people who have ownership status of a business are sometimes classified as being entrepreneurial and thus are static in that they continue to develop their business with little change. However, as Sarooghi et al. (2015) states that the process of generating and implementing ideas is riddled by contradictions, dilemmas, paradoxes and tensions. On the other hand the dynamic perspective focuses on how entrepreneurship is a process of change and creation that links in with creative solutions. Thereby the entrepreneur has energy that leads to the development of new ideas.

McDougall and Oviatt (2000: 902) suggests that "the domain of entrepreneurship overlaps with the domains of other constructs such as innovation, change management, and strategic management". This is important to developing sport entrepreneurship as a way to integrate different perspectives in the pursuit of business performance. Dzisi (2008: 256) suggests that the main personality characteristics of entrepreneurs are "commitment, determination and perseverance, the drive to achieve and grow, persistent problem solving, internal locus of control and innovativeness". These personalities are evident in sport entrepreneurs who link their passion for business with the sport context.

There are two main economic models to understand entrepreneurship: Kirzner and Schumpeter. Schumpeter (1934) viewed entrepreneurs as being innovators as they introduced new ideas into the economy. Dzisi (2008: 256) states "the main idea in Schumpeter's definition of entrepreneurship is an innovating entrepreneur who is the actor and translator of inventions and new ideas into commercial production".

Kirzner (1997) viewed entrepreneurship through a process of discovery potential in market processes. Dzisi (2008: 256) states Kirzner viewed entrepreneurship as a concept "that of alertness by individuals to profitable opportunities to gain pure profit". Both Schumpeter and Kirzner viewed the entrepreneur as being the important decision maker in assessing opportunities.

Drucker (1985) suggests that change can arise from (a) unexpected events, (b) incongruity, (c) process needs, (d) unforeseen changes, (e) demographics, (f) alterations in perception and (g) new knowledge. Unexpected events include changes in the way sport is played or viewed that have an impact. The internet has changed the way people watch sport with an increase in international viewership. Incongruity involves differences between the perceptions of reality. In sport there can be incongruity between the ability of athletes to perform and what coaches expect. Process need involves improving on current ways of doing things. In sport technology has improved the process of buying tickets through self-service online sites. Unforeseen changes involve developments in the way an industry is structured. In the sport industry, there is a lot of overlap between other sectors such as education and tourism that have meant the blurring of industry boundaries. Demographics involves differences in gender, age and living conditions. In sport, the ageing of the population and increased interest in lifestyle sports has given rise to an increase in slower sports such as yoga. Changings in meaning involve differences in the mood of individuals or the marketplace. New sport technologies such as fitness apps were first perceived as hard to use but this has changed due to increased user acceptance. New knowledge involves gaining information from different sources about potential opportunities. In sports medicine this new knowledge enables the development of innovative treatments and practices.

Johannisson (2014: 109) states "entrepreneurship is more concerned with hands-on action and social interaction that is aimed at envisaging and enacting new realities than on rational decision making". Sport has been used as a metaphor in strategic management studies to understand competitive behavior. This is evident in Drucker (1985) describing one strategy as entrepreneurial judo due to the need to defend and attack in the marketplace. The effects of the internet revolution and internationalization has forced sport organizations to become more entrepreneurial. In the era of advanced information and communications technology being integrated more into daily lives and business practices, the key driver of growth in sport is excelling in entrepreneurship. Sport helps create and foster entrepreneurship through participation and involvement in activities. This is due to sport being a natural environment for entrepreneurship due to its integration within many urban and rural communities around the world. For this reason, many sport organizations are pursuing entrepreneurship for competitive reasons.

The experiences of entrepreneurs influences the growth of business ventures, which are also affected by the economic and industry conditions. Thus, there are unique challenges for entrepreneurs who are involved in scientific discoveries from sport-based ventures. Increasingly technological advancements are influencing the actions of entrepreneurs. Beckman et al. (2012: 203) states that technology entrepreneurship "focuses on new ventures where developments in science or engineering constitute a core element of the entrepreneurial opportunity". The improved technology services available to sport organizations will continue to improve entrepreneurial endeavours. In addition, the internet and related social media have provided opportunities for consumers to participate in the creativity process in sport.

More sport organizations are encouraging consumers or fans to be part of the creativity process by suggesting new ideas. Wu et al. (2015: 263) defines consumer creativity as "the consumer's general ability to generate innovative ideas in the consumption context, and it includes two dimensions: novelty and usefulness". This creativity enables the feedback from consumers to be used in a positive manner to create new business ventures. In sport due to the loyalty and commitment to particular teams this creativity enables a generation of buzz around potential ideas.

5.4   Sport and Lifestyle Entrepreneurship

Sport is part of people's lifestyles and influences the development of entrepreneurship. Mont et al. (2014: 30) states that lifestyles "define, connect and differentiate us and they also influence and are influenced by institutions, infrastructures and environmental conditions". Sport is played in different ways along a continuum from accidental, committed, driven, incidental, and occasional to sporadic (Weed and Jackson 2008). Moreover, sport has a number of impacts on businesses and governments including community, economic, environmental, financial, health, international, promotional and sociocultural (Huggins 2013). The relationship between entrepreneurship and sport has become an important are of study in its own right.

Huggins (2013: 107) states "sport is a global, multibillion dollar industry, a dominant and defining force in millions of lives". Sport industries fuel the entrepreneurial development of countries and regions. Countries such as the United States are known for encouraging the growth of sport businesses such as Nike and Under Armour. Moreover, certain regions in the United States such as New York have a large number of sport teams that have fans around the world.

The sport industry is gaining more attention from entrepreneurship scholars due to its linkage to technological innovation. Pehkonen and Ikonen (2016: 1) states "sport is not only about competition between athletes but between different sports as well". Thus, there is a debate about how to define a sport due to its changing nature from technological advancements. A sport is normally defined by funding bodies, organizations and the media (Pehkonen and Ikonen 2016).

Post sports are categorized by "holistic, physical and cultural styles of life" (Pehkonen and Ikonen 2016: 3). In sport organizations these decisions involved evaluating the different types of innovation that may lead to an entrepreneurial business venture. This will help the entrepreneur develop a business plan with an appropriate timeline and resources. Thus, the involvement of key people who can trigger the creation of a sport venture is important.

5.5   Sport Entrepreneurship Research Dimensions

A sport enterprise is involved in sport and conducts some form of business activity. There are many similarities between a sport and normal enterprise as both are involved in revenue generating activities. However, the key difference is the orientation towards the health and fitness industry. Entrepreneurship has a demonstrably effect on sport organizations performance. However, there is a lack of understanding about how sport organizations can harness entrepreneurial capabilities. Thus, training and education is required to explore how entrepreneurial competences enhance entrepreneurship.

Entrepreneurship can be evaluated in different ways including financial and non-financial indicators. Financial indicators include "growth rates, business size, turnover, profitability, and the number of people employed" (Dzisi 2008: 257). In sport there are often easy ways to assess these financial indicators including ticket sales and merchandise spending at events. However, sport has a social and community side to it that makes it important to evaluate non-financial indicators. These include learning in a sports context that can be at the individual or team level. In addition, many people view sport as a way to achieve personal fitness goals. This means often entrepreneurship in sport is assessed through the creation of new ideas that involve self-fulfillment.

The involvement in sport entrepreneurship can occur at the individual or collective level depending on the environmental context. Individuals see new challenges that can be developed in sport. Often the charisma of individuals enables them to be expressive about potential new sport businesses. In order to be successful the individuals need to be dynamically involved and instrumental in the idea process. This requires commitment and the tasks needed to be performed and open to new challenges. At the collective level the involvement in sport entrepreneurship infers a group of people or organizations that are involved in the process. Collective entrepreneurship around sport can occur in an open or closed group context. The open context normally involves free and shared information about potential sport ideas. This open context is evident in user communities in an online environment that facilitates like-minded people to derive sport ideas. The closed group infers that the ideas have intellectual property or impacts on a sport's competitiveness. For those reasons often closed groups are used as a way to limit the spread of information about a sports innovation. Despite the emphasis on sharing new information there is a general concern that good ideas need to be trademarked and protected before they enter the marketplace.

Sport entrepreneurship needs to gain legitimacy by developing research from different contexts in order to point out subtleties. It is surprising that so little work has been conducted in the area of sport entrepreneurship. When designing sport entrepreneurship it is important to understand the context. Table 5.1 depicts the research design dimensions and issues in sport entrepreneurship. This is helpful in understanding how the analysis level, focus, methodology, purpose, theories and time are becoming important areas to study within sport entrepreneurship.

Table 5.1 Sport entrepreneurship research dimensions

Research design dimensions	Research issues
Analysis level	Individual, team, project
Focus	Culture, personality, process, social
Methodology	Case studies, explanatory, longitudinal
Purpose	Descriptive, exploratory
Theories	Practical, contextual
Time	Narrow, wide

Adapted from Low and MacMillan (1988)

5.6   Knowledge Infrastructures and Sport

Knowledge infrastructures include the way information about sport is shared that alters discourse about current practices. This is important in changing the rules and modernization of sport but it is important for sport managers to focus on the response of consumers to the innovation during the implementation stage (Harding et al. 2016). New sports such as surfing are becoming more mainstream due to their commercial appeal. These new sports are often innovative and part of the sport economy, which is linked to its continual growth.

Drucker (1985: 135) states that innovation "to be effective, has to be simple and it has to be focused". The acquisition of new knowledge is important in sport in order to increase socioeconomic development. However, there is some instability in the sports marketplace due to the new knowledge from technological innovations that is disrupting the marketplace. Thus, some large sport organizations have eroding market share due to the emergence of new sport ventures that bypass traditional business models.

The existence of an entrepreneurial mindset enables sports organizations to develop innovations that will facilitate new growth areas. Sports organizations that have a deep knowledge of innovations can create better customer value. This helps turn innovation into sustainable growth and facilitates better economic progression. Thus, increasingly entrepreneurship is viewed as a way for sports organizations to be more competitive as they shift attention to new areas. The significant value for sports organizations is that innovation enhances overall growth and potential for future change.

Rivera (2017) defines innovation through both customer satisfaction and value. Customer satisfaction involves responding to the needs and wants of customers in a responsive manner whilst customer value involves creating value in a new way to customers. Rivera (2017: 139) states that entrepreneurship involves "contending with independent entrepreneurs in novel markets to create new customer value". This interaction in sport is needed to facilitate the flow of information about potential business ventures.

There are new methods of obtaining sources of innovation including contests, design thinking and incubators (Mirvis et al. 2016). Innovation in sport comes from a range of sources including enterprises, government policy and social entrepreneurs. McKelvey and Zaring (2017: 1) states that a social innovation "is a novel activity or organizational mode that is not, or at least not primarily, motivated by private gain or business logic". Increasingly social forms of innovation are becoming evident in new business ventures that link corporate social responsibility to sport teams.

5.7 Sport Leadership and Entrepreneurship

The ambidexterity theory of leadership for innovation proposes that both closing and opening behaviours are needed (Rosing et al. 2011). The creation of innovation in sport often includes conflict between those wanting change and those wishing to keep the status quo. Sarooghi et al. (2015) states that "an ambidexterity perspective argues that the conversion of creative ideas into innovations involves potentially conflicting activities and imposes potentially conflicting demands on individuals, teams and organisations". The ambidexterity perspective of innovation is a useful way to understand the benefits but also pitfalls of engaging in sport entrepreneurship. Thus, some knowledge needed to generate ideas may involve competition for scarce sport resources. Sarooghi et al. (2015) suggests three main forms of ambidexterity that are important to generating innovation. These are temporal ambidexterity that involves the same organization performing activities at different times. Structural ambidexterity involves different organizations performing activities whilst contextual ambidexterity is focused on behaviors and the situation surrounding the innovation.

Both closing and leadership behaviours are needed to evaluate ambidextrous leadership. Closing leadership behaviours are defined as "leader behaviours that reduce variance in follower behaviours by taking corrective actions, setting specific guidelines, and monitoring goal achievement" (Zacher and Rosing 2015: 55). In sport corrective actions might involve improving existing practices to provide better services. Setting specific guidelines means having processes in place for sport innovation that detail the steps needed for change. Monitoring goal achievement refers to how the sport innovation develops then feeds into the market.

Opening leadership behaviours are defined as "leader behaviours that increase variance in follower behaviours by encouraging them to do things differently and to experiment, giving followers room for independent thinking and acting and supporting followers attempts to challenge the status quo" (Zacher and Rosing 2015: 55). As many sports have rigid requirements about player behavior it might be hard to do things differently. However, many innovations have occurred in clothing and equipment that are outside the rules of the game. Independent thinking in sport is helpful in deriving new ideas and forms of behavior. This is connected to changing the status quo in terms of current behavior in sport. Examples of this include increasing gender diversity and equity in sport.

Sport policy makers can benefit from entrepreneurship research as it suggests ways to better impact societal development. This is crucial in the global economy that needs innovation in order to bring about more competition. Leaders in sports teams can facilitate innovation by coming up with new ideas that create better outcomes. This is important as implementing new ideas in sport involving changing routines. This theory is useful as a way of explaining the different ways innovation is developed based on leadership qualities. In sport, coaches can encourage players to experiment with new ideas in order to facilitate new playing practices. Sport leaders that enable errors as a way to learn can develop new innovative behaviours. Mascia et al. (2015: 102) states "innovation is a social activity where communication and interaction play important roles". This social activity involves networks and relationships that play an important role in sport entrepreneurship.

Exploitative activities in organizations involve the execution and implementation of ideas (Zacher and Rosing 2015). Sport organizations need to make sure they implement innovation in a way that lends itself to positive change. Explorative activities in organizations mean the experimentation and search for innovation that results in a competitive advantage (Zacher and Rosing 2015). More research attention is needed on the drivers of innovativeness in sport organizations performance. Innovativeness determines the competitiveness of the sport sector as it is a way of meeting new needs in the marketplace. Organizations that have a culture of openness are able to facilitate the introduction of new ideas. Figure 5.1 depicts the sport innovation resources and capabilities. The resources are divided into cognitive, intellectual, relational and structural. These resources affect the capabilities of sport organizations to develop innovation in terms of development, ideation and marketing.

5.8   Sport Team Cohesion

Team cohesion is an important part of the innovation process particularly in a sports context as there are naturally many different types of teams. Carron et al. (1998: 213) definite team cohesion as "a dynamic process that is reflected in the tendency for a group to stick together and remain united in the pursuit of its instrumental objectives and/or for the satisfaction of members affective needs". In sport there are teams put together to play one another in a formal context but there are also informal teams such as the fans of the sport. In addition, there are teams of supporters for specific sports that watch and follows a particular sport. Thus, the context of teams in sport will change depending if they are amateur or professional in composition. Generally team cohesion in both amateur and professional contexts is based on group members sharing a common goal.

The relationship between members of a sport team will impact on their ability to be innovative. In sport, there has been a trend towards globalization of teams that has meant a growing international market for sport products and services. Team members that work well together can perform tasks more effectively making collaboration easier to achieve. This cohesion enables innovation to develop that helps improve a sport team's competitiveness. As the sports market is global and very competitive it means team cohesion is a way of enabling opportunities to come

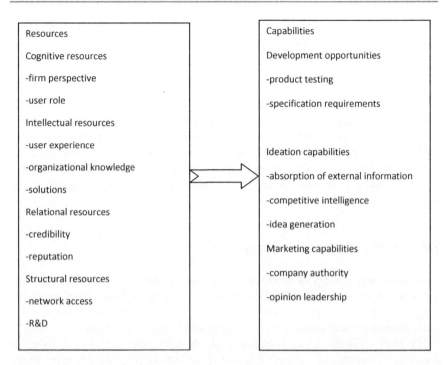

Fig. 5.1 Sport innovation resources and capabilities. Adapted from Schweisfurth and Herstatt (2014)

to fruition. This global competitiveness drives innovation and makes sport organizations change their strategies.

Team cohesion facilitates an inter team climate that fosters the flow of information (Efrat et al. 2017). This interteam climate enables information to be disseminated and processed in a way that allows others to understand its impact. Trabal (2008: 313) states "the dialogue between the sporting world (athletes, trainers, technical staff) and that of research scientists into performance is a difficult one". For innovation to succeed this climate needs to be receptive to the ways people communicate information. Sport teams that adapt based on information received are better able to coordinate their innovation.

There are prosocial behaviours of sports teams such as secrecy and teamwork that create a bonding culture (Halldorsson et al. 2017). Halldorsson et al. (2017: 1) states that teamwork involves "transforming an aggregate of skilful individuals into a coordinated and cooperative social group". In sport there are different functions members of a team have depending on their skills. Some teams will have more important members that are required as part of the coordination process. However, in order for a sports team to function properly they need to be cooperative in the form of leadership. This is due to individuals in a team having certain personality characteristics that influence behavior.

Many sports are based on teamwork that influences innovation in terms of sharing experiences and influencing creativity. Zacher and Rosing (2015: 56) define team innovation as "a team's capability to generate novel and original ideas (i.e. creativity) as well as the capability to put these ideas into practice such that they yield beneficial outcomes (i.e. implementation)". The teamwork culture affects that sense of shared achievement and willingness to be innovative. Some sports teams have a natural inclination to be innovative as it is embedded in the joint spirit of the group members. Thus, sport teams that engage with the innovation process are likely to be more successful. The team culture in sport means that there is a sense of solidarity.

5.9   Collaborative Economy

There are a large number of sport teams that are increasingly using online technology as a way to be part of the collaborative economy. Sport teams have consumer tribes that follow particular teams, athletes and series. Consumer tribes can be entrepreneurial when innovations developed lead to new opportunities (Canniford 2011). Most consumer tribes utilize multiplicity as membership of other tribes is allowed and freedom of expression is part of the membership requirements. Playfulness is another characteristic as it encompasses a sense of fun and enjoyment as being a member of the tribe. This is important in facilitating innovation as a sense of playfulness leads to creativity. Transience refers to changes from people and resources that make group membership dynamic (Canniford 2011). Sport has a sense of transience that is part of the competitive nature of the industry.

In an online environment there are collaborative innovation processes performed by individuals and teams that help influence sport entrepreneurship. This helps people share tasks and improve information flows in a global environment. In addition, there are global sport interest online communities that enables the integration of ideas and enhances the flow of knowledge. In the past innovation was considered a sequential process that involved deliberate action within an organization. This conceptualization of innovation has changed with the evolvement of faster markets that have a more disordered process. Innovation is now considered a chaotic and complex process that is hard to observe (Barnes and Mattsson 2016).

E-tribes are groups of people who communicate through the internet. In sport there are many e-tribes around particular teams and for specific types of sport. These e-tribes are involved in user innovation as they discuss and develop new ideas. This is due to the internet transcending typical physical boundaries that enables easier and quicker communication. Many of these sport e-tribes have a high degree of emotional involvement in the online process as they are passionate supporters. Moreover, e-tribes have also been referred to as virtual communities of practice due to the group activity in an online context (Dube et al. 2005). This is evident in sport e-tribes developing innovations that help their team or sport

Table 5.2 Sport and collaborative communities

Characteristic	Examples
Community goals	Altruistic: for the benefit of society
	Commercial: financial reasons most important
Extent of controls	Low: informal collaboration
	Medium: volunteered interaction
	High: forced joint activity
Shared values	Market driven: based on market need and capacity
	Pro-social: focused on social needs

Adapted from Barnes and Mattsson (2017)

develop better capacities. Table 5.2 states the different types of tribes that exist in sport in terms of their characteristics and examples.

5.10 Conclusion

This chapter has discussed the way entrepreneurship is essential for sport organizations to survive in their competitive environment. Entrepreneurship and sport are intimately related due to the reciprocal nature of competitiveness. In this chapter, I have looked into the determinants of entrepreneurship within a sports context. This chapter suggests that sport entrepreneurship needs to be understood based on cultural, historical and technological connections. This chapter has synthesized the literature by providing some recommendations for fostering sports entrepreneurship: (1) be creative by thinking outside the box, (2) challenge existing business models by developing new ones and (3) create an innovation climate by taking risks. In addition, this chapter has suggested that more interest should be applied to lifestyle entrepreneurship in sport. More assistance is needed for sport entrepreneurs who have the potential to significantly affect societal developments. With the background of entrepreneurship in mind, the role of this chapter was to emphasize the need for innovation in sport. This enables business practices to develop that support entrepreneurship in sport.

References

Audretsch, D. B., Kuratko, D. F., & Link, A. N. (2016). Dynamic entrepreneurship and technology-based innovation. *Journal of Evolutionary Economics, 26*, 603–620.

Barnes, S. J., & Mattsson, J. (2016). Building tribal communities in the collaborative economy: An innovation framework. *Prometheus, 34*(2), 95–113.

Beckman, C. M., Eishenhardt, K., Kotha, S., Meyer, A., & Rajagopalan, N. (2012). The role of the entrepreneur in technology entrepreneurship. *Strategic Entrepreneurship Journal, 6*, 203–206.

Canniford, R. (2011). How to manage consumer tribes. *Journal of Strategic Marketing, 19*(7), 591–606.

Carron, A. V., Brawley, L. R., & Widmeyer, W. N. (1998). The measurement of cohesiveness in sport groups. *Advances in Sport and Exercise Psychology Measurement*, 213–226.

Drucker, P. F. (1985). *Innovation and entrepreneurship*. New York: Harper & Row.

Dube, L., Bourhis, A., & Jacob, R. (2005). The impact of structuring characteristics on the launching of virtual communities of practice. *Journal of Organizational Change Management, 18*(2), 145–166.

Dzisi, S. (2008). Entrepreneurial activities of indigenous African women: A case of Ghana. *Journal of Enterprising Communities: People and Places in the Global Economy, 2*(3), 254–264.

Efrat, K., Gilboa, S., & Yonatany, M. (2017). When marketing and innovation interact: The case of born-global firms. *International Business Review, 26*(2), 380–390.

Halldorsson, V., Thorlindsson, T., & Katovich, M. H. (2017). Teamwork in sport: A sociological analysis. *Sport in Society.* https://doi.org/10.1080/17430437.2017.1284798

Harding, J., Lock, D., & Toohey, K. (2016). A social identity analysis of technological innovation in an action sport: Judging elite half-pipe snowboarding. *European Sport Management Quarterly, 16*(2), 214–232.

Huggins, M. (2013). Sport, tourism, and history: Current historiography and future prospects. *Journal of Tourism History, 5*(2), 107–130.

Ireland, R. D., & Webb, J. W. (2007). A cross-disciplinary exploration of entrepreneurship research. *Journal of Management, 33*(6), 891–927.

Johannisson, B. (2014). Entrepreneurship: The practice of cunning intelligence. In *Swedish Entrepreneurship Forum: 20 years of entrepreneurship research* (pp. 109–119).

Kirzner, I. M. (1997). Entrepreneurship discovery and the competitive market process: An Austrian approach. *Journal of Economic Literature, 35*(1), 60–85.

Knight, F. (1921). *Risk, uncertainty and profit.* Boston: Houghton Mifflin.

Low, M. B., & MacMillan, J. (1988). Entrepreneurship: Past research and future challenges. *Journal of Management, 14*(2), 139–161.

Mascia, D., Magnusson, M., & Bjork, J. (2015). The role of social networks in organizing ideation, creation and innovation: An introduction. *Creativity and Innovation Management, 24*(1), 102–107.

McDougall, P. P., & Oviatt, B. M. (2000). International entrepreneurship: The intersection of two research paths. *Academy of Management Journal, 43*(5), 902–906.

McKelvey, M., & Zaring, O. (2017). Co-delivery of social innovations: Exploring the university's role in academic engagement with society. *Industry and Innovation.* https://doi.org/10.1080/13662716.2017.1295364

Mirvis, P., Herrera, M. E. B., Googins, B., & Albareda, L. (2016). Corporate social innovation: How firms learn to innovate for the greater good. *Journal of Business Research, 69*(11), 5014–5021.

Mont, O., Neuvonen, A., & Lahteenoja, S. (2014). Sustainable lifestyles 2050: Stakeholder visions, emerging practices and future research. *Journal of Cleaner Production, 63*, 24–32.

Nambisan, S. (2017). Digital entrepreneurship: Toward a digital technology perspective of entrepreneurship. *Entrepreneurship Theory and Practice, 41*(6), 1029–1055.

Pehkonen, S., & Ikonen, H.-M. (2016). Too good to be a sport? Why dog agility struggles in gaining recognition as a sport. *International Review for the Sociology of Sport*, 1–17.

Ratten, V. (2011). Sport-based entrepreneurship: Towards a new theory of entrepreneurship and sport management. *International Entrepreneurship and Management Journal, 7*(1), 57–69.

Rivera, M. J. (2017). Leveraging innovation and intrapreneurship as a source for organizational growth. *International Journal of Innovation Science, 9*(2), 137–152.

Roberts, K. (2017). Sport in Europe's era of austerity: Crisis or adaptation? *International Journal of Sociology and Social Policy, 37*(1/2), 123–130.

Rosing, K., Frese, M., & Bausch, A. (2011). Explaining the heterogeneity of the leadership-innovation relationship: Ambidextrous leadership. *Leadership Quarterly, 22*(5), 956–974.

Sarasvathy, S. D. (2001). Causation and effectuation: Toward a theoretical shift from economic inevitability to entrepreneurial contingency. *Academy of Management Review, 26*(2), 243–263.

Sarooghi, H., Libaers, D., & Burkemper, A. (2015). Examining the relationship between creativity and innovation: A meta-analysis of organizational, cultural, and environmental factors. *Journal of Business Venturing, 30*(5), 714–731.

Schumpeter, J. A. (1934). *The theory of economic development.* Cambridge, MA: Harvard University Press.

Schweisfurth, T. G., & Herstatt, C. (2014). How internal users contribute to corporate product innovation: The case of embedded users. *R&D Management, 46,* 107–126.

Thiel, A., & Mayer, J. (2009). Characteristics of voluntary sports clubs management: A sociological perspective. *European Sport Management Quarterly, 9*(1), 81–98.

Trabal, P. (2008). Resistance to technological innovation in elite sport. *International Review for the Sociology of Sport, 43*(3), 313–330.

Weed, M., & Jackson, G. (2008). The relationship between sport and tourism. In B. Houlihan (Ed.), *Sports and society.* London: Sage.

Welter, F., & Lasch, F. (2008, March). Entrepreneurship research in Europe: Taking stock and looking forward. *Entrepreneurship Theory & Practice,* 241–248.

Wu, J., Wen, N., Dou, W., & Chen, J. (2015). Exploring the effectiveness of consumer creativity in online marketing communications. *European Journal of Marketing, 49*(1/2), 262–276.

Zacher, H., & Rosing, K. (2015). Ambidextrous leadership and team innovation. *Leadership & Organization Development Journal, 36*(1), 54–68.

Sport Business and Entrepreneurship

6

6.1 Introduction

Sport has an experiential component as people like to watch games and feel the atmosphere. Pehkonen and Ikonen (2016: 4) states "sport is defined in terms of physical education and exercise that produce well-being and public health benefits". Sport has evolved to be seen as a professional career option that utilizes business strategy in the pursuit of increased performance. Burnes and O'Donnell (2011: 13) states "sport, like business, is highly competitive, and success depends on continuously striving to outperform the opposition". Sport can be categorized as organized when there is a competitive and regulatory structure to it or unorganized as it has a non-competitive and more recreational or leisure goal (Spaaij and Westerbeek 2010). The role of leaders in sport such as coaches has changed in line with more emphasis on entrepreneurial behaviours. This is reflected in traditional coaches being authoritarian but modern ones as empowering and well educated (Burnes and O'Donnell 2011). Thus, there has been a change to a more participative style of sport leadership that values innovation.

Wakefield (2016) suggests that there are four ways to understand passion in sport: heart, mind, body and soul. The heart involves the love of sport that continues despite the performance of a team or athlete. The heart perspective can range in intensity depending on the level of love for the sport. The mind involves the psychological association with a sport. This means assessing the amount of time spent thinking about a sport. The body involves the physical associations with a sport. This can involve spending time watching a sport or participating in activities related to a sport. The soul component is about the degree of feeling whether an individual can live without. This means asking questions about the importance of sport in the life of an individual.

Individuals have passion for sport that affects the amount of money and time spent on sports products and services. This means that there is often a high value associated with sport that impacts entrepreneurship. Governments and individual's judge sport as being more important than other activities due to the passion associated with sport. This means that there can be more effort spent on sport due

© Springer International Publishing AG 2018
V. Ratten, *Sport Entrepreneurship*, Management for Professionals,
https://doi.org/10.1007/978-3-319-73010-3_6

to the perceived values for society. Sport is valued as an important activity and associated with people's identity. There is an emotional part of sport that is linked to whether a person feels passionate. This is due to some individuals having an inclination to engage in sport due to them feeling it is important. Thus, sport passion involves people investing time in this activity due to the benefits it brings them.

This chapter demonstrates two important components of the development of sport-based entrepreneurship theory. First, the application of existing entrepreneurship theories to the sport context can provide a better way to understand change. This provides more structure to the future theoretical application of sport entrepreneurship. Part of this process is to examine the assumptions and applications of existing entrepreneurship theory to sport. This will involve aligning current theoretical processes to a sport context. Second, using theory from business management about entrepreneurship can facilitate a faster progression about the distinctiveness of sport entrepreneurship. Thereby enabling entrepreneurship and business management scholars to contribute to the development of the field of sport entrepreneurship.

Studies about sport entrepreneurship can provide new insights about the application and management of change within sport. Research into sport entrepreneurship will continue to increase in future years. While the study of entrepreneurship processes has been central to business management researchers, it has been backgrounded in sport management research. More business researchers are focusing on entrepreneurship as a way to understand change and evolution in the industry. Thus, bringing entrepreneurship theory into sport can usefully inform our understanding about how existing and emerging sport organizations build their competitiveness.

6.2 Popularity of Sport in Society

Sport organizations account for a part of the global economy and influence other areas of society. Whilst the popularity of sport in society is undeniable there is little understanding about the role of entrepreneurship in sport and its impact on economic performance. This has resulted in an incomplete understanding of sport entrepreneurship and how it is distinct from other types of entrepreneurship. Often sport organizations might be performing well but their unique funding and capabilities need to be understood in terms of their market performance. Thus, unfortunately the nature of entrepreneurship in sport is still debatable due to the ignorance about the level of innovation occurring in a sports context. This is partly due to a lack of understanding about how to define a sport business due to the large number of hybrid organizations that meld sport to both the profit and non-profit business context. The objective of this chapter is to uncover the role of sport and sport organizations in the entrepreneurship process. There is evidence that the link between sport and entrepreneurship is being more noticeable due to the technological changes occurring. Traditionally the entrepreneurship discipline has focused on understanding the development of new businesses whilst sport management has focused on the environmental context in which sport occurs.

Sport is practiced in solitude or with a group of people (Borgers et al. 2016). In addition, there are changes in culture that have led to an increase in sports that have more flexibility in terms of their roles and style of play. Morrison (2000: 62) defines an entrepreneurial culture as "an expression of an attitude towards commerce at a business level". The sport industry has an entrepreneurial culture due to its need to be receptive to new opportunities. This comes from changing demands of consumers about sport products and services.

Culture is a way people interpret the world and sustains human behavior (Morrison 2000). Culture is vital to understanding the role individuals play in shaping entrepreneurial action. Hofstede (2002) in a seminal study of culture stated that there were five dimensions: power distance, individualism, masculinity, uncertainty avoidance and long term orientation. A culture of entrepreneurship can be established through recruiting people with new ideas and the establishment of teams that focus on innovation. To achieve an entrepreneurial culture there needs to be the introduction of innovation programs that facilitate creativity through new market developments.

Culture is an important way to understand entrepreneurial approaches and the role of societal attitudes towards business activity. The effectiveness of entrepreneurship may be related to behaviours deemed as more acceptable in certain cultures such as risk taking activity. However, most entrepreneurs regardless of their culture exhibit the same behavioural traits such as imagination and the seeing of possibilities. These traits are important due to the leadership, persuasive and problem solving activities that entrepreneurs play in society. Seltsikas and Lybereas (1996) states that process theories involve focusing on what entrepreneurs do, their position within class structures. This means there is an emphasis on the personality of the entrepreneur in terms of how their inherent psychological behavior such as risk taking aptitude influences behavior.

There sometimes needs to be a distinction between the entrepreneurial behaviours of males and females in a sport context. Whilst there is increasing recognition of gender neutral sport policies there is still some differences, which effect entrepreneurial behavior. Shaw and Hoeber (2003: 351) states "male athletes are portrayed and perceived as tough hard players who rarely express emotions other than aggression and anger, and only smile to celebrate victory". These characteristics typify the male stereotypes about how they should behave in sport based on their gender. Thus, gender has a role in sport and is often marketed as a defining characteristic. Some athletes capitalize on this masculinity in their clothes and way they play on the field. In football, tattoos are common on players and are considered as a sign of masculinity in some cultures. The loud and domineering characteristics sometimes associated with male athletes are often considered as good behaviors in sport. However, with increased emphasis on the role of females in sport these attitudes are changing. Shaw and Hoeber (2003: 351) states that "women play the role of cheerleaders, who are perceived by the viewer to be feminine and glamouress, exhibiting cheerful emotions and glittering smiles".

Thus, whilst male athletes are respected for behaviours associated with anger, female athletes are considered better if they act in a positive manner.

There has been entrepreneurship in new sporting forms emerging in the market-place. Sports such as skateboarding that were considered informal sports have become more accepted due to the changing ideology in society. This is due to more people acknowledging sport as a form of entrepreneurship and way to express themselves through creation ways that sport is conducted. In the case of skateboarding the use of inner city office buildings provided a way for skateboarders to make use of their environment. In addition, empty swimming pools that were not being used for swimming were converted into skate bowls thereby being utilized for another sport. In the past sport was considered adventurous and linked to leisure activities. The traditional values of teamwork and collective concern were endemic in the traditional sports of hiking and tennis. However, as more people live in urban areas there has been a use of sport as an escapism mechanism to everyday life. Thus, sport in many urban areas has been utilized as a form of rebellion as it supports individualism. This is made more evident in cultural lifestyle movements that encourage newness and innovation, which are characteristics of entrepreneurship.

Sport is a highly competitive industry due to its continuous change and growth. The value orientation towards more autonomy and informal practice of sport has meant lifestyle sports have increased (Borgers et al. 2016). Lifestyle sports such as walking or hiking are emerging in different forms due to the changing way people interact with their environment. This is seen in the free to use sports environments such as parks being utilized for sports pursuits. Moreover, there has been an increased interest in healthy lifestyles that has fueled interest in specific sports such as yoga becoming more popular. Sport is seen as a freedom mechanism to be sometimes reckless but in a socially acceptable form. This enables sports communities to develop as they enable the pursuing of self-expression. Sport is increasingly seen as a way to engage in a contemporary social life through physical activity.

The delivery of sport has changed "from the one-to-many, single-medium frame-work of sport consumption traditionally offered by television to the many-to-many possibilities of internet-enabled sport participatory consumption" (Pegoraro 2014: 2). This change has resulted in sport consumers obtaining information from a variety of sources at multiple time periods. Social media is one of the most used new technology innovations as it has changed the way communication about sport occurs. Social media enables an interaction between people in the form of creating a community through instant communication. This communication can occur between fans but also via athletes and teams sharing information. This has enabled a more cost and time effective way to communicate about sport that has constantly changed with the introduction of new mobile applications such as Facebook and Twitter.

The nature of sport has changed due to historical events including industrializa-tion, the internet revolution and urbanization. This has meant sport is largely affected by society trends that affect its evolution and development. Much of the change in the sport industry has been driven by the constant need for competitiveness. The similarity between sport and business is often reflected in the way teams are structured and managed. This is evident in professional sport teams but can be seen in amateur clubs that pride themselves on their competitiveness. Thus, sport has parallels to business due to the use of different kinds of people in the management structure. This is reflected in specialists including dieticians, doctors, physiotherapists and trainers (Burnes and O'Donnell 2011). Increasingly there has also been the use of data analytics in sport to analyze potential strategies similar to that conducted in organizations. This was evident in books including Moneyball about Oakland Athletics, the baseball club and their use of data analytics to recruit players despite having little financial resources.

There is an emphasis on winning in business that is similar to that occurring in sport. Thus, both amateur and professional forms of sport emphasise the role of team cohesiveness and coordination in the pursuit of winning a game. For sport leaders to succeed they need to utilize business strategies such as scenario planning in order to project future behavior. In order for there to be successful leadership in sport there needs to be an ability to manage and develop talent. Chelladurai (1990) proposed that in a sports context the performance and satisfaction is influenced by leader behavior. Thus, the required actual and preferred behavior of a sports leader is affected by the sports context.

There are antecedents affecting the behavior of sport leaders. This includes the characteristics of the situation from amateur to professional coaches, who might be motivated by different factors. Some sport coaches might focus more on enjoyment of the game for all team members rather than performance. However, the situation is also affected by weather and playing conditions. Leader characteristics is another antecedent of leader behavior. In Chelladurai's (1990) model of sport leadership some leaders are team builders and focus on improving both mental and physical performance. Other leaders prefer teaching athletes through experiential learning and on field performance. The other antecedent is member characteristics, which includes the type of sport being played. There are both profit and surplus seeking sport businesses that have different leadership and organizational styles. This is depicted in Table 6.1.

6.3 Development of Entrepreneurship

Etemad (2016: 159) states "the origin of the term entrepreneurship is attributed to the French economist, Jean-Baptist Say, defining contemporary French wine traders as entrepreneurs in early eighteenth century". The definition of entrepreneurs is changing as there are evolving ways to conduct business depending on the market context. Harding (2006: 7) defines entrepreneurship as "any attempt at new businesses or venture creation, such as self-employment, a new business organization or the expansion of an existing business by an individual, team of individuals or established business". In order to start ventures there needs to be a determination of the resources needed and how they can be acquired.

Table 6.1 Types of sport business

Profit seeking sport business	Surplus seeking sport business
Non-government sport media corporations	Development organizations
Privately or shareholder owned sporting franchises or teams	Elite sport training institutions
Sport consulting companies	Government owned media companies
Sport event companies	Government policy agencies
Sport manufacturing companies	Sport governing bodies

Adapted from Spaaij and Westerbeek (2010)

Entrepreneurs are self-motivated individuals who start enterprises relying on their initiative (Mueller and Thomas 2000). Entrepreneurs are distinguished from other business people due to their ability to implement their visions. Other characteristics of entrepreneurs relevant in a sport context are confidence in their ability to develop a business. This means they have the resourcefulness to obtain necessary ingredients to start a business. Sometimes this means having a tunnel vision about how they see the future success of a business. An important component of entrepreneurial behaviour is the way they organize economic and social mechanisms for their advantage (Hisrich 1990). This can involve high intensity and energetic conduct about the future potential of their behaviour.

The practice based view of entrepreneurship "advocates a process-oriented and contextual-based view of co-creation" (Maritz and Donovan 2015: 79). There are processes involved in developing an entrepreneurial venture in sport from the initial thinking about an idea to developing it into a commercial venture. In this process there are a number of steps and decisions an entrepreneur needs to make in order to have an outcome. In addition, there are alternative ways sport entrepreneurship can develop that depend on the level of knowledge needed to progress the business venture. This is dependent on the context of the proposed sport venture that might need certain resources. Thus, some entrepreneurship in sport will be due to the co-creation between individuals, government and businesses. This co-creation involves managing the knowledge from the ideation stage, which is dependent on the level of risk and return from the sport venture.

Entrepreneurs need to be risk takers as they go after opportunities in pursuit of business growth. Thus, they have a self-realization that their endeavours will bring about change in the marketplace. For the reason, they are seen as independent and sometimes mavericks due to their different kind of behavior compared to others in the marketplace. In order to prosper entrepreneurs need to have a determination that their beliefs will lead to business development. An entrepreneur has a personal vision but also is a social agent. Sport entrepreneurs utilize their personal vision to link a business idea to a sport environment. This involves focusing on the opportunities existing in the sport space that are facilitated by interpersonal interactions. Most sport entrepreneurs utilize information flows to derive business ideas.

There are many different reasons individuals become entrepreneurs including "the desire for independence and control, family tradition, to improve social status, and the motivation to innovate, and create new products" (Sriram et al. 2007: 238). Most definitions of entrepreneurship focus on the formal sector but the informal part is also important. Pathak et al. (2016: 2) states that the informal economy is controversial as it is referred to in different ways such as the "shadow, hidden, black, underground, gray, clandestine, illegal and parallel economy". In the sport industry, the informal economy plays a role in producing and selling products that are illegal. The gap between the formal and informal economy is debatable depending on the country context due to the different ethical and social norms.

The unit of analysis in entrepreneurship can be at the individual, organizational or team level. Athletes or sport managers engage in entrepreneurship as a way to differentiate themselves and gain a competitive edge. Sriram et al. (2007: 247) states that "entrepreneurship works best when it bubbles up from individual initiative". At the organizational level sports teams or societies are involved in entrepreneurship to gain monetary or political power. Williams (2007: 35) states that "commercial entrepreneurship is increasingly becoming more socially orientated as manifested in the rapid emergence of greater corporate social and environmental responsibility".

Morrison (2000) suggests that the cultural dimensions supporting entrepreneurial behavior are: communal versus individual; conformist versus divergent; and equal versus elitist. In sport there are communal cultures existing in team sports that require cooperation amongst individuals. However, this communal culture is also influenced by individual cultures in terms of personality characteristics. This is increasingly evident in athletes being international celebrities and having their own social media accounts. The conformist culture in sport means that most sports teams require the wearing of the same clothes as part of their membership requirements. In addition, there are formal and informal codes of conduct that necessitate a conformist approach in sport. There is some divergent behavior that involves athletes behaving differently. In most sports there are equal rules applied to sport that all athletes must adhere to. However, there are some elitist sports such as golf that require more money to play and thus are only available to certain segments of the population.

6.4 Sport Business and Entrepreneurship

Studies about sport entrepreneurship are flourishing due to the realization that sport is inherently entrepreneurial. For entrepreneurship to progress there needs to be some form of knowledge that is recognized as a potential business opportunity. Much of the entrepreneurship in sport is conceived in another industry then used in a sports context. Thus, the process of entrepreneurship often involves exploiting knowledge in another environment that is then modified to suit the sport industry. Connecting the fields of sport and entrepreneurship is important in creating a body of knowledge about sport entrepreneurship. Often entrepreneurial behaviours of sport organizations come from the competitiveness of the industry. Thus, sport entrepreneurship is created from the linking of the sport, business and entrepreneurship fields. There is a tendency to ignore the role of entrepreneurship in sport.

The entrepreneurial process is complex and dynamic in sport and initially it involves creating ventures that can be profit or non-profit in orientation. Sport entrepreneurship is a field of its own and differs from other types of entrepreneurship. Thus, there needs to be more encouragement about how to delve deeper into this field of research.

There has been only recently a development in the field of sport entrepreneurship due to the diversities and contexts of sport. The term 'sport' has changed over the years as different types and purpose have evolved. The actual practice of sport entrepreneurship has been around for a long time since humans started linking sport to business ideas. There is a contemporary trend towards emphasizing the technological innovations in sport as entrepreneurship. In the past, prior to the advent of the internet, sport entrepreneurship meant selling new sports related products and services. The dynamic nature of sport during the past decade when linked to e-commerce has meant that different types of businesses have emerged. There has tended to be a lag between the actual practice of sport business and the scholarly literature related to entrepreneurship. This is partly due to the fast changing business environment in sport where new ideas are quickly put into practice. I believe that a focus on sport entrepreneurship will contribute to a better theory that utilizes the fields of entrepreneurship and sport management.

Taking an entrepreneurial view of sport provides an important way to consider the rationale and processes of sport. The sport entrepreneur is at the center of an interactive environment that thrives on the dissemination of knowledge. However, there are some contradictions in the way entrepreneurship relates to the development of new products and processes in sport. This is due to the limited understanding of the way entrepreneurship is managed in sport and the continued emphasis on competitiveness. In addition, there has been comparatively little academic attention paid to sport entrepreneurship compared to other types of entrepreneurship.

Sport entrepreneurship has raised the attention of academics, practitioners and policy planners due to its role in the knowledge economy. There is an increasing pace of technological development that is escalating interest in entrepreneurship for sport professionals. The need for entrepreneurship in sport should be addressed exclusively from an economic and financial point of view. A complementary reason that considers the social relationships in entrepreneurial ecosystems should be taken into account. These social elements are important ways of transforming society through establishing new connections.

Sport entrepreneurship provides a significant strategic direction for all types of organizations involved in sport. The immediate benefit of entrepreneurship in sport is the focus on actions required to stay competitive in the long term. Entrepreneurship provides a meaningful way organizations can incorporate innovation into their strategic thinking. Entrepreneurship generates innovation in a range of ways through increased visibility and being proactive about future developments. Entrepreneurial leadership is important to sport organizations due to inspiration being a way to motivate others. Sport organizations that are considered market leaders tend to engage in new product development in order to maintain their competitiveness.

Sport entrepreneurship theory gives opportunity to focus on the role of innovation in the development of a business. In practice, a sports entrepreneurship approach facilitates competitiveness and innovative ideas by combining available resources with futuristic thinking. Sport entrepreneurs require resilience and often patience in making ideas become practice. This involves creativity but also fortitude about focusing on market conditions for the best performance. Some sports have cultural conditioning that impacts behavior. There is a tendency for group thinking and conforming to expected behavior in many team sports. Thus, cultural attitudes in sport can be communal and limit innovation. This means that there can be an obligation to look after other members of a team rather than focusing on individual needs. To incorporate innovation in sport teams there may be an intuitive response based on projected change. This means that some members of a sport team tend to enjoy the game rather than suggesting new ideas. There may also be negative connotations associated with voicing an opinion in a sports team due to the role of group consensus. This can influence the low tolerance for failure if the idea is not accepted in a positive way. In light of the emphasis on entrepreneurship in society, sport entrepreneurship offers a way to integrate sport into the discussion.

6.5   Sport Networks

Sriram et al. (2007: 242) highlights how "entrepreneurs seek resources through their social networks regardless as to whether the ties are weak (acquaintances) or strong (close friends)". Sport networks involve a group of people connected by interpersonal ties or shared interests. Entrepreneurs utilize these networks in order to cultivate contacts that can help develop an idea. This means that people who have experience or knowledge about sport can be utilized to facilitate reciprocal interaction about ideas. Hence, the mutual trust that exists in a sport network will be more of an obligation to help sport networks as sources of information that facilitate the development of business networks.

There are cultures within certain sports that influence behaviors and values. Some sports such as football have certain attitudes that are part of their culture, which influence entrepreneurship. This means that certain sports have a more entrepreneurial culture that leads them to behave in different ways. Lifestyle sports favour a more informal culture that enables more innovation. Formal sports such as cricket have rigid rules that lead to less innovation.

Sport entrepreneurship uses networks as the locus of innovation in order to build new market products and services. There is interaction between networks and the cyclical process of re-iteration that progresses ideas to action. Cooperative networks exist in sport as a way of facilitating the exchange of information. There are positive and negative aspects of cooperative networks in sport. The positive aspects involve focusing on how there is a mutual interdependence between entities that generates alliances to help develop sport ventures. The negative aspects are the dependent relationships that may exist in sport due to the government and regulatory restrictions. This means that intermediary organizations help develop the cooperative networks when there may be regulatory restrictions.

Social networks are important for entrepreneurs and they include "advisors, business partners, buyers, customers, employees, friends/relatives, investors, mentors, shareholders, and suppliers" (Klyver and Grant 2010: 213). Entrepreneurs have social networks that are evolving depending on the stage of their business ventures (Klyver and Grant 2010). The resources needed for business ventures differs at each stage of a business venture, so there will be a reconfiguration in their social relationships. From an entrepreneurs social networks they can gain information and knowledge needed to establish credibility in their businesses. Often these social networks help to cement the reputation of an entrepreneur by providing advice and skills required in order to establish the legitimacy of the business.

Sport entrepreneurship arises from the interlocking activities that involve multiple stakeholders. There is a stereotype of entrepreneurs acting by themselves in a maverick fashion. This means that sport entrepreneurs tend to be characterized as non-conforming in their quest to establish business ventures. This is crucial in enabling sport entrepreneurs to be relentless in their pursuit of business success. The perception of entrepreneurs as single individuals underestimates the value of teams and groups in the entrepreneurship process. This is more pronounced in sport entrepreneurship as there is often a need for commitment from other entities. Thus, the message emerging from the many successful sport entrepreneurs is that there needs to be collaboration between stakeholders in order to succeed. Thus, the producer of entrepreneurship in sport is the community of individuals and organizations interested in the process.

The resource based view is a useful way to understand the competitiveness of sport businesses. In the resource based view, resources are a way of understanding entrepreneurial activities and their impact on business outcomes. Sport organizations have to manage their resources in a way that enhances their competitiveness. The resource based view is helpful in identifying the characteristics of sport organizations that are different to other types of organizations. The identification of distinctive capabilities of sport organizations can help improve our understanding of the role sport plays in the global economy. In addition, there needs to be more awareness about how the resources of sport organizations help enhance their performance.

In the resource based view social capital provides a valuable resource and a way to develop business ventures. Often social capital is embedded in the sport industry due to the social networks existing that enables access to information and resources. In order to be entrepreneurial there needs to be access to information about potential opportunities. Networks influence business success through community and government ties that are endemic in the sport industry. When there is more environmental uncertainty social networks provide a way to access information that can provide a competitive advantage.

Networks vary in strength depending on the backgrounds shared by individuals. There is increased business advantages when networks are utilized to provide a relationship lubricant that makes it easier to do business. It is often necessary to utilize networks with political leaders and government officials to facilitate the growth of new sport ventures. This is due to the need for sport entrepreneurs to acquire institutional support. To assess the success of new sport ventures there needs to be an evaluation of the network benefits. Often individuals in sport have personal attributes such as being competitive and proactive that are essential characteristics for entrepreneurship. To stimulate sport venture creation there needs to be networks in particular regions or industries that provide a benefit for the individuals involved.

6.6 Entrepreneurial Ecosystems

Audretsch and Belitski (2017: 1033) defines an entrepreneurial ecosystem as "a dynamic community of inter-dependent actors (entrepreneurs, suppliers, buyer, government etc.) and systems level institutional, informational and socioeconomic context". There are institutionally embedded actors in sport that form part of the entrepreneurial ecosystem. The creation of new sport ventures depends on the ability of entrepreneurial ecosystems to allocate resources through the interaction with other actors. Often the perceptions about a new sport venture will depend on the ability to access information and knowledge with the networks of an ecosystem.

Due to the increase in online sports games, the ecosystems can occur in an electronic or physical formal. For the ecosystems to generate new ideas about sport there needs to be some form of entrepreneurial action. In sport due to the systemic regulation the ecosystems help to foster new ideas. Audretsch and Belitski (2017) argue that there is an increasing need for information technology to align with individual decision making in entrepreneurial ecosystems. This helps to create better ways to analyse entrepreneurial risk and evaluate opportunities. For many sport entrepreneurs the ability to foresee changes in the environment is a way they become competitive.

The future success of many sport organizations comes from the way they integrate entrepreneurship into their business practices. This helps build aspirations about the value of entrepreneurship in sport. The historical experiences of many organizations comes from their openness to incorporate new business practices. The entrepreneurial culture in sport organizations may require thinking about how to maintain tradition while incorporating change. Some sport clubs including well known international ones have utilized entrepreneurship but in a negative manner. This is reflected in the sports doping cases and illegal use of club money to fund other action. The positive aspects of entrepreneurship are being incorporated more into sport as a way to foster a better culture. Any explanation of the positive and negative aspects of entrepreneurship need to come from an understanding about the role of change in sport. This ensures there is respect about how sometimes entrepreneurial cultures need to be managed.

Choices involve the alternative way of conducting entrepreneurship from establishing a business or setting up a franchise structure. In sport, there are both profit and non-profit organizations that are established for different reasons. Some people still view sport as a non-profit or community activity but this has changed with the increased professionalization of sport. Thus, there is a degree of subjectivity about how to view business activities in a sport context. This has led to some creativity in the use of resources for sport ventures. Van de Ven (1993: 212) states that ideal entrepreneurs "possessed the creative labor, vision of a business idea, antagonism of non-innovative administrators, investment selection skills to hire capitalists, and risk taking capacities to strike out into the unknown". Table 6.2 states the dimensions of entrepreneurship.

In a seminal book Wallas (1926) proposed that the creative process involves five stage: preparation, incubation, insight, evaluation and elaboration. Preparation involves finding ways to introduce new ideas and ways of thinking. In sport it includes using fabrics in clothing or utilizing new technology. The incubation stage involves developing the idea by focusing on the required ingredients needed to make it a success. Insight involves obtaining feedback and advice from other people in terms of how the idea will work. This can involve thoughts about the future of the sport industry in terms of changing needs. Evaluation involves focusing on the negative and positive aspects of the idea. The evaluation process can utilize athletes to test ideas to see if there is a practical application. Elaboration involves progressing the idea past its initial stage to develop different products or services.

Table 6.2 Entrepreneurship dimensions

Dimension	Examples
Choices	Alternatives Subjectivity Creativity Resources
Exploitation	Scarce resources Innovation
Entrepreneurial process	Venture creation Resource determination Resource acquisition Venture development Managing the growing business Scalability Sustainability Harvest
Opportunity identification	Idea generation Context Perception interpretations
Unit of analysis	Individual Organisationa Team

Adapted from Maritz and Donovan (2015)

The highly regulated structure of many sports leagues means that there are limited choices in how to expand or innovate within sport. Exploitation involves using scarce resources in a way that benefits an individual or organization. Sport fields and facilities are often under-utilized due to events occurring at night or on weekends so the introduction of new usages will enable these resources to be better utilized. Sometimes it might involve exploiting the sport resources in an innovative way. This can include sport stadiums being used for entertainment or other reasons.

6.7 Opportunity Recognition in Sport

Opportunity recognition involves generating new ideas for sport products, services or processes. This will involve focusing on how the context of sport is changing from including more individual sports that focus on lifestyle reasons. For example, the perception of sports by consumers such as yoga and surfing changed from being adventure to mainstream forms of recreation. This has come about from the interpretation of what a sport is and means changing in society. Most definitions of entrepreneurship focus on opportunity recognition in terms of evaluation, exploitation and identification. Opportunity recognition in sport often emerges from new technologies being introduced into the marketplace then adapted to suit the sport environment. Rubleske and Berente (2017: 132) states a pragmatist perspective of opportunity recognition is defined as "a dynamic and unfolding experience which an entrepreneur conceives as a general market need and tries to exploit for financial or social gain". The focus on creativity means that opportunities are socially constructed from their environment.

Rubleske and Berente (2017) states that opportunity recognition can take a constructivist or discovery view. In the constructivist view opportunities emerge as creative ways to engage in business activity. Thus, depending on the progress of technological innovation some opportunities may be cognitively evaluated depending on the circumstances. In sport opportunities are often based on an entrepreneur having a proactive attitude about future trends. This means they can foresee a product being used in a sports context and find resources in order to make it a reality. Thus, sport entrepreneurs are dynamic leaders who see a gap in the marketplace. This is important in facilitating the cognitively way opportunities are created. Thus, in sport some opportunities will be based on athlete or player behavior. For example, the need for sweat resistance material or lightweight running shoes. The discovery view suggests that opportunities are waiting to be found. This means that people just need to find these opportunities, which can occur anywhere. Often opportunities result from information asymmetries that enable business ventures to develop.

The entrepreneurial aspects of sport are an important component as they lead to the development of new products, processes and technologies. Opportunities for new sport products are often conceived within an organization then exploited in other environments. The evolving field of sport entrepreneurship is modifying over time. Sport is an effective vehicle for introducing entrepreneurship. The diverse characteristics of the sport environment require further developments to account for entrepreneurship. More sport facilities are being outsourced to private providers as a way for governments to earn money. The reason for this change in the management of sport centers is partly due to the need to incorporate different types of sports. For example, indoor rock climbing is a popular activity for people living in inner city areas due to the locational advantages of the sport centre. Throughout the history of sport it has constantly evolved to suit the environment.

6.8   Sport Innovation

Sport innovation is co-created through a network of stakeholders that emphasizes the dynamic nature of the industry. Innovation as a field of study has tended to separate the innovators or producers from the customers or adopters (Vargo et al. 2015). Most of the innovation research emphasises the technology parts and less on the market roles. This is due to technology influencing organizations and product development based on consumer demands. Innovation can be diffused into the market in a strategic manner that emphasizes outcomes. The wider environment of the sport industry from the political and social systems plays a role in facilitating or hindering entrepreneurship. This is due to sport organizations being embedded often both in the private and public sectors of economic ecosystems.

Nambisan and Baron (2013: 1071) defines an innovation ecosystem as "a loosely interconnected network of companies and other entities that coevolve capabilities around a shared set of technologies, knowledge, or skills, and work cooperatively and competitively to develop new products and services". The continued interaction of sport organizations in society impacts the degree of innovation. Modular innovation is defined as "putting things together in new ways" (Scaringella and Burtschell 2017: 154). This form of innovation is helpful in managing complex organizations and projects that require thinking differently about strategies. For innovation to gain traction it needs to be developed beyond its initial state through the involvement of individuals or teams. In some sports organizations it may be hard to implement innovation due to the bureaucracy and hierarchical structure. Often hierarchical organizations are not conducive to innovation due to the lack of a collaborative work culture. This has led to the suggestion that less rigid and more flexible organizational structures that promote cooperation are needed to implement innovation.

Organizations that have a good communication system may be able to share and disseminate ideas about innovations. Thus, the structure of an organization is an important part of the implementation process for innovation. Innovative organizations are those with less layers of hierarchy, which can facilitate employees to be empowered and take ownership of ideas. Therefore, organizations that are less centralized and have a more level organizational structure are likely to implement innovation at a faster rate.

Entrepreneurial capacity in sport organizations can be achieved by devoting more time and resources to innovation. There has been a trend out of competitive team sports into individual sports. This is due to more focus in society on individuals and their needs rather than working together in a team. In the past most sports were played in a team environment on playing fields subsidized by governments. There was more emphasis on amateur sports played on weekends at the end of the work week but due to changing work hours more individual-based sport is occurring. Fitness gyms that have indoor facilities have grown particularly in urban areas due to people working at night and on the weekends.

6.9   Future Developments in Sport Business

The focus on the sport aspects of entrepreneurship has economic consequences as it concerns the business role sport plays in society. The new variation of entrepreneurship in sport can make a difference to the entrepreneurship discipline in terms of connecting other subject areas.

Entrepreneurship efforts within the sport industry have received more attention in the media and academic literature in recent years. This chapter has provided a better understanding of how sport entrepreneurs behave in the marketplace. The general impression is that sport entrepreneurs have a distinct emotional attachment to sport that distinguishes them from other types of entrepreneurs.

Sport entrepreneurship research has a long way to go in terms of developing a comprehensive body of research that incorporates different types of entrepreneurship. There needs to be more discussion between sport management and entrepreneurship researchers in order to gain new perspectives. Defining sport entrepreneurship is a challenge for researchers due to the existence of different interpretations. Sport entrepreneurs have unique attitudes about the role sport plays in business. This means that entrepreneurship in sport is valued in different ways depending on the circumstances. Sport entrepreneurs often behave in a certain fashion due to the need to be seen as a market leader. In order to understand sport entrepreneurship there needs to be an acknowledgement that individuals have different ambitions for being entrepreneurs. Some sport entrepreneurs have a predisposition to entrepreneurship due to their competitive nature and association with sport. This means there are individuals who value sport entrepreneurship based on their inclination to undertake business ventures. Sometimes entrepreneurship is viewed as culturally desirable in sport due to the need for increased performance outcomes. Entrepreneurship in sport can be exercised as a way of dealing with environmental constraints such as funding. In addition, the absence of certain sport products provides a way for entrepreneurs to enter the market and fill a gap. This enables more mobility towards sport entrepreneurs facilitating market development.

In the entrepreneurship literature there has been a tendency to focus on general definitions rather than those specific to an industry. Sport entrepreneurs have tended to be missing in studies of entrepreneurship. Uncovering the role entrepreneurship plays in sport represents an important contribution to the general entrepreneurship literature. Although there is considerable overlap between sport entrepreneurship and generalentrepreneurship, they have different characteristics. Not all sport business ventures are entrepreneurial as they remain in the same business throughout their lifetime. Sport entrepreneurs are characterized by their preference for innovation thereby distinguishing themselves from managers or business owners. It is suggested that the manifestation of innovation in sport entrepreneurship is a key trait. Current studies of entrepreneurship have neglected sport in the research. This has led to a focus more on well-known types of entrepreneurship such as international or social. This has meant a lack of understanding about the sport environment and its entrepreneurial characteristics.

There has not been much work done on entrepreneurship in sport in contrast to entrepreneurship studies in other fields. More researchers need to view sport entrepreneurship as an understudied but useful are where they can apply business management frameworks. There needs to be more sport entrepreneurship researchers adopting useful business management theories in order to generate knowledge. This will help substantiate sport entrepreneurship as a unique area of business management research. Thus, the use of multiple theoretical frameworks that complement each other to understand sport entrepreneurship is required. This is due to there being multiple strategies for the rationale behind developing entrepreneurship in sport. Future research should be addressed about how sports institutions in terms of how the environment and policy affect its development. This book demonstrates that it is worthy to focus on sport entrepreneurship in different contexts.

6.10   Conclusion

In closing, there is a major conclusion that is heralding an era of new sport organizations: the relatively large number of new sport startups that are focusing on entrepreneurship. This chapter has shown that consideration should be given to entrepreneurship in sport. Future investigations about the nature of sport entrepreneurship need to view both commercial and social rules as equally important in understanding its development. The outcome of this chapter is that it will encourage future research to unravel the concept of sport entrepreneurship. This is important due to the increasing amount of technological innovations being introduced into sport so there needs to be research about how organizations and public policy planners can respond. This chapter provides an opportunity to find out more about sport entrepreneurship. One of the most obvious ways sport is entrepreneurial is the addition of new businesses and technology to the industry. From a business perspective, entrepreneurship produces significant benefits for sport organizations that can cooperate with other stakeholders to build entrepreneurial business ventures.

This chapter serves as a way of highlighting the gaps in the literature and areas of potential future study. Moreover, this chapter contributes to the theory of sport entrepreneurship in two ways. First, it focuses attention on the distinctive characteristics of sport organizations. Second, it incorporates a behavioral component that has not been discussed before. This chapter makes a compelling argument that sport organizations play an important role in economic and social wealth creation.

References

Audretsch, D. B., & Belitski, M. (2017). Entrepreneurial ecosystems in cities: Establishing the framework conditions. *The Journal of Technology Transfer, 42*(5), 1030–1051.

Borgers, J., Pilgaard, M., Vanreusel, B., & Scheerder, J. (2016). Can we consider changes in sport participation as institutional change? A conceptual framework. *International Review for the Sociology of Sport,* 1–17.

Burnes, B., & O'Donnell, H. (2011). What can business leaders learn from sport? *Sport Business and Management: An International Journal, 1*(1), 12–27.

Chelladurai, P. (1990). Leadership in sports: A review. *International Journal of Sport Psychology, 21*(4), 328–354.

Etemad, H. (2016). International entrepreneurship as a young field of scholarly inquiry and its relationship with the knowledge network of five related disciplines. *Journal of International Entrepreneurship, 16,* 157–167.

Harding, R. (2006). Entrepreneurs: The world's lifeline. *Business Strategy Review, 17*(4), 4–7.

Hisrich, R. D. (1990). Entrepreneurship/intrapreneurship. *American Psychologist, 45*(2), 209–222.

Hofstede, G. (2002). The pitfalls of cross-national survey research: A reply to the article by Spector et al. on the psychometric properties of the Hofstede values survey module 1994. *Applied Psychology, 51*(1), 170–173.

Klyver, K., & Grant, S. (2010). Gender differences in entrepreneurial networking and participation. *International Journal of Gender and Entrepreneurship, 2*(3), 213–227.

Maritz, A., & Donovan, J. (2015). Entrepreneurship and innovation: Setting an agenda for greater discipline contextualisation. *Education & Training, 57*(1), 74–87.

Morrison, A. (2000). Entrepreneurship: What triggers it? *International Journal of Entrepreneurial Behavior & Research, 6*(2), 59–71.

Mueller, S. L., & Thomas, A. S. (2000). Culture and entrepreneurial potential: A nine country study of locus on control and innovativeness. *Journal of Business Venturing, 16,* 51–75.

Nambisan, S., & Baron, R. A. (2013, September). Entrepreneurship in innovation ecosystems: Entrepreneurs self-regulatory processes and their implications for new venture success. *Entrepreneurship Theory & Practice,* 1021–1097.

Pathak, S., Xavier-Oliveira, E., & Laplume, A. O. (2016). Technology use and availability in entrepreneurship: Informal economy as moderator of institutions in emerging economies. *The Journal of Technology Transfer, 41*(3), 506–529.

Pegoraro, A. (2014). Twitter as disruptive innovation in sport communication. *Communication & Sport,* 1–6.

Pehkonen, S., & Ikonen, H. M. (2016). Too good to be a sport? Why dog agility struggles in gaining recognition as a sport. *International Review for the Sociology of Sport.* https://doi.org/10.1177/1012690216679834

Rubleske, J., & Berente, N. (2017). A pragmatist perspective on entrepreneurial opportunities. *International Journal of Innovation Science, 9*(2), 121–136.

Scott, A. J. (2006). Entrepreneurship, innovation and industrial development: Geography and the creative field revisited. *Small Business Economics, 26,* 1–24.

Scaringella, L., & Burtschell, F. (2017). The challenges of radical innovation in iran: Knowledge transfer and absorptive capacity highlights—evidence from a joint venture in the construction sector. *Technological Forecasting and Social Change, 122*(1), 151–169.

Seltsikas, P., & Lybereas, T. (1996). The culture of entrepreneurship: Towards a relational perspective. *Journal of Small Business and Entrepreneurship, 13*(2), 25–36.

Shaw, S., & Hoeber, L. (2003). 'A strong man is direct and a direct woman is a bitch': Gendered discourses and their influence on employment roles in sport organizations. *Journal of Sport Management, 17,* 347–375.

Spaaij, R., & Westerbeek, H. (2010). Sport business and social capital: A contradiction in terms? *Sport in Society, 13*(9), 1356–1373.

Sriram, V., Mersha, T., & Herron, L. (2007). Drivers of urban entrepreneurship: An integrative model. *International Journal of Entrepreneurial Behavior & Research, 13*(4), 235–251.

Van de Ven, A. (1993). The development of an infrastructure for entrepreneurship. *Journal of Business Venturing, 8*, 211–230.

Vargo, S. L., Wieland, H., & Akaka, M. A. (2015). Innovation through institutionalization: A service ecosystems perspective. *Industrial Marketing Management, 44*(1), 63–72.

Wakefield, K. (2016). Using fan passion to predict attendance: Media consumption and social media behaviours. *Journal of Sport Management, 30*, 229–247.

Wallas, G. (1926). *The art of thought.* New York: Harcourt-Bruce.

Williams, C. C. (2007). Socio-spatial variations in the nature of entrepreneurship. *Journal of Enterprising Communities: People and Places in the Global Economy, 1*(1), 27–37.

System Processes in Sport Entrepreneurship

7

7.1 Introduction

Sport industries include a range of businesses such as fitness centers, sports clubs to recreational facilities. This diversity in type of sport business means that there are different processes involved in the formation, maintenance and growth of entrepreneurship. Sport industries are central to cultural and economic development but whilst there is increasing interest in entrepreneurship as an important part of the global economy, little research has explicitly investigated the sport industry. This is perhaps due to the changing types of sport from traditional to more adventure focused growing in the industry. Pehkonen and Ikonen (2016: 3) distinguishes between traditional sports as being goal orientated and rule governed with post-sports focusing on emotional and physical aspects.

Spaaij and Westerbeek (2010: 1361) states "sport can be used to foster new friendships and social connectivity across class, religious and ethnic boundaries". Some research has focused on the role of entrepreneurial processes to the success of sport organizations, but the research is still inconclusive about its effects. The process of sport entrepreneurship often starts in small sport clubs then as it gains traction gets incorporated into larger sport clubs. Historically many sport organizations have not had to be entrepreneurial due to government or community funding. This has changed in recent years with more attention on public/private partnerships that enable cooperation with funding methods.

Sport organizations have a competitive advantage since they are involved in competition as part of their business structure (Comeaux 2013). This means that the entrepreneurial development process in sport requires different forms of participation. Borgers et al. (2016: 638) states "sports participation behavior can be considered as a choice or as an expression of individual motives, attitudes, preferences or abilities". This focus on participation is due to sport generally relating to fun and enjoyment whilst business management is about evaluation. Thus, sport can be less formal and of a more fluid nature. Borgers et al. (2016: 640) define non-club organized sport as "participation in health and fitness centres, extra-curricular sports programmes, facilities offered by municipalities and private companies as

© Springer International Publishing AG 2018
V. Ratten, *Sport Entrepreneurship*, Management for Professionals,
https://doi.org/10.1007/978-3-319-73010-3_7

well as to self-organized participation in informal groups or alone". This results in business management of sport needing formal procedures in order to manage the performance of an organization (Pinch and Henry 1999). Sport entrepreneurs utilize both sport and business principles in order to create a synergistic effect.

Entrepreneurship enables sport organizations to be self-sufficient by generating additional revenue through the implementation of new processes. The world of entrepreneurship focuses on ways to be creative in business, which is important for sport organizations (Madrigal 2000). Sport entrepreneurship is a promising strategy to address problems and issues in sport. The widening disparities between social and commercial reality for many profit and non-profit sport organizations has meant more focusing on entrepreneurship. Sport organizations are being encouraged to become more entrepreneurial, innovative and self-reliant. Moreover, sport is being subjected to more commercialization, whereby business ideologies are reproduced in organizations. This means that the politics and structure of sport organizations are shifting to an entrepreneurial paradigm. In the context of sport entrepreneurship, scholars are focusing on business approaches in technology and internationalization. The competition amongst sport organizations is evident in more being entrepreneurial with funding and policy initiatives.

Entrepreneurship has been the main way sport has developed and evolved over the past decade. Entrepreneurial activity has advantages for the sport industry including economic, social and technological. In the globally connected world entrepreneurship is increasingly important. Sport entrepreneurship can include incoming and outgoing forms of innovation processes, which affect firm behavior. Incoming entrepreneurship involves how sport organizations integrate new thinking and processes into their business structure. This helps them advance technology by integrating advances from other fields into the sport context. Outgoing entrepreneurship involves sport organizations innovating and this includes processes affecting other industries. This has been a way the sport industry has been integral to the development of other industries such as education and tourism.

This chapter contributes to the intersection of research on sport and entrepreneurship by providing guidance and information about the role of processes. This chapter is based on two drivers of sport entrepreneurship-orientation (willingness to act) and capability (aptitude to act). Both these actions are part of the way sport organizations manage the entrepreneurship process.

7.2   Literature Review

7.2.1   Entrepreneurship

Entrepreneurship is important in the business environment as it is associated with non-linear dynamics and rapid change (Zhao 2005). To capture ideas there needs to be a way to link the theory to a practical setting through the application of entrepreneurial processes. There has been a trend towards viewing entrepreneurship as a concept and process rather than as purely involving small business management

(Haugh 2005). This is due to entrepreneurship being associated with innovation that needs knowledge in order to design concepts. To be an entrepreneur there needs to be a rational decision maker who assumes risk and manages the process (Morrison 2000). The entrepreneurial portion of the sport sector usually wields a disproportionate influence on the economy. Most conceptualizations of entrepreneurship involve innovation in a business management setting but it can also occur in other settings including within government and non-profit organizations. This is due to entrepreneurs exploiting the value of ideas in a business context, which requires the focus on contextualizing the process.

Conventional entrepreneurs seek to enter business sectors that are already in existence in a way that is similar to current business practices. These entrepreneur values influence their career and structure of sport organisations. The management both of an organization to run efficiently whilst being entrepreneurial can be a source of conflict. This is due to the time pressures in running a business meaning managers may have difficulty in developing entrepreneurship. In addition, the day-to-day running of the business becomes more important than entrepreneurship. The time demands from a business may leave little time for managers to focus on innovation and creativity. However, one of the most important aspects of a manager's job is their ability to be entrepreneurial. The decision to change can have a big impact on an organization and on a manager. When a manager decides to be entrepreneurial then market dynamics come into play that requires decisions to be made.

Entrepreneurship is socially constructed based on the environment in which it occurs. This means that entrepreneurship needs to be understood as something related to society. It is envisioned that entrepreneurship inevitably involves both a social and business element depending on its context. Therefore, entrepreneurship occurs in combination with the environment and can open up a number of possibilities. This is due to the web of processes that sport entrepreneurship needs to evolve.

7.2.2 Sport Business

The importance of sport business is recognized globally in terms of job creation. Sport businesses generate wealth for additional industries and services. Research about sport entrepreneurship is progressively including more disciplinary perspectives that enable a holistic understanding of the topic. Entrepreneurship is socially constructed and is reflected in attitudes towards innovation. The field of sport entrepreneurship can be explored by taking an interdisciplinary stance towards the construction and use of innovation. Suggested areas of study needed to advance research on sport entrepreneurship involve focusing on types of innovation. This means that there are some habits of sport organizations needing to change in order to understand the entrepreneurship process. This involves focusing on the procession view of sport entrepreneurship and the ongoing flux of change. There are two main schools of thought in the formulation of entrepreneurship theory: micro view and macro view (Provasnek et al. 2017).

This is due to the intentionality placed on competitiveness and the performance of the sport organization. Sometimes though there can be a problem due to the intersection of two systems, the sport and the management of the business. These systems can be incompatible due to different values placed on each.

There are various types of management styles that sport enterprises can utilize. This includes acting in a stable and conservative manner to limit risk. Other styles include being a maverick or change agent that focuses on disrupting the status quo. Furthermore, there are social dynamics that come into play making it complicated for sport entrepreneurs. Dealing with government and other regulatory bodies may be in contrast to the sport entrepreneurs need for autonomy and independence. However, government controlled state entities are also engaging in entrepreneurship as a way of innovating their organizations. This is occurring due to the anticipation of ownership changes or a trend towards more self sufficiency in sport organizations.

There are different members of the value chain for a sports organization that will effect entrepreneurship planning and they include customers, managers, suppliers, fans and players. Each of these members may view entrepreneurship in a different way depending on their position in the organization. Due to the multiple and different interests of these stakeholders the level of entrepreneurship planning will alter, often to the detriment of the sports organization. By proactively engaging in entrepreneurship planning this can help sport organizations focus on the future.

To understand the future of sport there needs to be more strategic thinking around entrepreneurship. Entrepreneurship is a process rather than one time event and has different stages in its development that sport organizations need to manage. These include the development stage when an idea is shared amongst key stakeholders. Afterwards there is the coordination stage that requires resource and time allocation. Lastly there is the marketing stage, which advertises the new product or process to others in and outside the organization. There are often power struggles within sport organizations that need to be resolved or managed with regards to entrepreneurship. This is due to generally the result of people in sport organizations having different ideas about progress. Some people have different goals, needs and expectations about their organization. This may influence the harmony within an organization and be reflected in the lack of willingness to change. To motivate more people to see the benefits of entrepreneurship the process needs to be properly managed.

The relationships of the key decision makers are the most important for entrepreneurship. Once the process of entrepreneurship begins there needs to be more coordination amongst stakeholders in the sports organization. This is a complex affair as there are a myriad of issues to grasp. As the field of sport entrepreneurship moves forward there are other issues relating to theory, policy, practice and teaching that need to be addressed. The reasons for a successful sport organization have altered in recent years due to the importance of entrepreneurship in their development. Increasingly entrepreneurship in different forms such as innovation have enabled sport organizations to adapt and change to new market conditions. There is also acknowledgement about how other types of organizations can learn from sport organizations in terms of their business development. This is evident with words such as winning, team and performance being used in a business setting.

7.2.3 Sport Innovation Processes

Innovation needs to be managed properly in order to see it being implemented properly in the marketplace. This involves the integration of knowledge into a sport sector. There are idiosyncratic structures in sport organizations, which affect accountability norms. Sport organizations need to develop unique resources that can influence the innovation processes and outcomes. Knowledge integration involves the process of translating new knowledge into a sport business context. The nature of the global innovation process has changed due to shifts in geographies, organizations and technologies. Sport organizations adopt innovations at different rates, which influences the diffusion process. There are different techniques for implementing innovation and these include pioneering breakthroughs in the marketplace. Many original ideas need to be path breaking in order to gain credibility amongst organizations in an industry.

Innovations can be categorized as administrative or technological. Administrative innovations include changes in the allocation of resources that impact the way an organization functions. This means policies often change when administrative innovation takes place and changes the structure of an organization. Technological innovation normally impacts the outputs of an organization by implementing new engineering ideas. Innovation is part of sport entrepreneurship but is a step needed before a business develops.

Entrepreneurship in an organization is influenced by the intentions and resources available for innovation. The willingness of sport organizations to innovate is influenced by their goals and motivations. Sport organizations need to be able to allocate resources to innovation. This adds to the entrepreneurial behavior and performance of the organization. There are different options available for sport organizations in terms of directing resources to innovation. This includes the strategic objectives and power associated with entrepreneurship. A tactic for many sport organizations is to focus on competitive and market conditions that influence innovation. Therefore, entrepreneurial sport organizations' have the ability to adapt behavior to suit emerging market conditions. Sport organizations due to their structure and ownership have almost unfettered discretion to innovate compared to other types of organizations.

Sport organizations' based on their unique competition are often more willing to experiment, which can cause entrepreneurship. However, there can be an aversion to innovate in sport organizations due to non-economic goals. This means they can be less innovative due to the unwillingness of managers to engage in entrepreneurial strategies. Given the importance of entrepreneurship to sport it is a wonder how these organizations' survive. This can be explained partly due to the other factors influencing sport organizations such as regulatory issues. Nevertheless sport organizations should be encouraged to be more entrepreneurial in order to tackle some of the emerging innovations entering the marketplace.

Sport organizations' need to have entrepreneurial absorptive capacity to design and manage knowledge. This includes strategic planning about how to deploy innovation in an organization in order to manage it properly. Sport organizations can take a portfolio management approach to design creative ideas. This enables entrepreneurship to be a tool for sport organizations to commercialize their innovations. The purpose of using entrepreneurship can be to help launch new ventures. Entrepreneurship involves the sport organization using their networks in order to involve the creation of value.

Sport entrepreneurs have a mindset of engaging in value creation through innovative activity. This indicates that the sport entrepreneur plays a role in evaluating and engaging in risk taking behavior. A growing interest in the business community is learning from successful sport entrepreneurs in how they developed their business. To do this it is important to understand the associations between sport and entrepreneurship. This helps to optimize the role sport entrepreneurs are having in society. Often entrepreneurship in sport is based on risk taking activity that can be a balancing act between innovation and the reality of doing business.

There has been a tendency for some to view entrepreneurship as easily conducted in sport organizations but often this is not the case. Entrepreneurship takes time to develop and there needs to be attention placed on its processes. This perception of entrepreneurship has puzzled some sport entrepreneurs who view entrepreneurship as needing a web of collaboration. Hence, sport entrepreneurship theorists argue that there needs to be a consistent and dynamic engagement of entities in order to make the entrepreneurship process work properly. These processes incorporate a range of activities such as business practices to styles of management in sport organizations.

Sport organizations combine the values and expectations of the sport with an organizational focus. This means that there may be context specific aspects of sport organizations that need to be considered when evaluating their entrepreneurial performance. Sport organizations are likely to handle entrepreneurship different compared to other types of organizations due to their focus on competition. There is a lack of agreement on how sport organizations are entrepreneurial. This ambiguity comes from the sometimes difficult way to understand the entrepreneurship occurring in sport organizations. It is anticipated that increasingly sport organizations will realize the entrepreneurial element of their business. Advice to sport managers about entrepreneurship must take into account the unique context of their organizations in the marketplace. For instance, many sport organizations have a hybrid financial structure with private and public funding, which affects their ability to be entrepreneurial. This means that context is an important way to understand an entrepreneurial perspective in sport. Therefore, sport organizations are an important type of organization in the global landscape due to their effect on individuals and other industries. This is due to sport entrepreneurship referring to at least three factors: first, the sport context; second, the processes involved in the innovation; and third, the knowledge needed to produce the change. Thus, the design of sport entrepreneurship will be based on business, political and environmental influences.

7.2.4 Evolving Entrepreneurship

Sport entrepreneurship tends to evolve based on decisions made about how to progress in the marketplace. This trajectory involves assessing possibilities to see how they will fit into the marketplace. There are different avenues a sport entrepreneur can take depending on their objectives. Sometimes the sport entrepreneur needs to see if they have the necessary resources in order to progress in the marketplace. This can take time depending on the adoption or understanding about the new product or process. Sport organizations are in an intense competitive environment that requires constant change to meet market needs. The drive for entrepreneurship usually comes from top management of a sport organization but sometimes also from customers and employees. There needs to be a long term view of entrepreneurship in sport organizations in order to have an open attitude about change. This means exploring how a new product or process will progress based on need and likeability in the market.

An ideal management style for entrepreneurship should be supportive and facilitate change based on feedback. This means entrepreneurship should be nurtured in a way to facilitate development. Entrepreneurship is a holistic process that requires an organizational culture that facilitates change. There is a diverse spectrum of views about entrepreneurship in sport and the relationship between them. A trend in the study of sport entrepreneurs has been towards how it differs compared to other types of entrepreneurship. This is due to sport entrepreneurship including new skills that enable an organization to operate in a different way. Thus, talent management of athletes has become a way sport organizations can be entrepreneurial. As part of talent management there is an emphasis on human capital and forms of behavior. Often athletes can be entrepreneurs due to the creativity of styles of play or performance. The creativity of an athlete involves capturing an opportunity in a sports context. This can include the athlete adding value to a sports organization in a way that has not been done before. Often athletes are entrepreneurial in informal ways that makes it hard to evaluate. This includes suggestions an athlete makes to their team about changes that involve innovation.

The internet is a way sport organizations are co-creating innovations with fans and customers. This involves a process of collaboration as the internet makes it easier to be interactive and involve more people in the feedback process. The internet and associated technology such as mobile commerce has transformed the sport industry into a more flexible and receptive environment for entrepreneurship. New technology has provided a way for more customer engagement in sport product innovation. This is conducted in an online mechanism that enables customer engagement in the co-creation process. The internet is a virtual environment that is often partnered with the physical environment in terms of linking to a sports organization. The internet has enabled sport organizations to implement a social dimension into discussions about team performance but also new product development. This has meant virtual communities have developed as a way for sport fans to participate in the innovation process. Individuals can choose their level of involvement in the innovation process depending on interests and time availability. This can be modified as the sport innovation process progresses and enters the marketplace.

Competition is an important element in the sport industry and affects the actions of organizations. The structure of the sport industry is due to the number of similar organizations targeting the same customers in an area. Sport organizations base their decisions on competitiveness within their industry, which is dynamic and constantly evolving. It is important for sport organizations to identify their main competitors and utilize market knowledge in order to increase their performance. Part of this competitive rivalry is due to the reaction of other organizations in terms of their movements in the market.

7.2.5   Sport Competitiveness

Sport organizations compete with other types of organizations particularly those in the entertainment industry for consumer spending. There are different customer segments that sport organizations compete for including consumers, business and government. This has resulted in sport organizations changing their market model to suit the degree of competitiveness in the industry. Entrepreneurship is a way sport organizations can express their creativity and innovation in the marketplace. The needs of sport organizations are often represented in their entrepreneurship, which is viewed not just as a desire of sport organizations but as a necessity in the marketplace.

The decisions about entrepreneurship are bounded by the constraints related to the sport organization. In addition, the characteristics of the innovation mean sport organizations need to monitor the entrepreneurial activities of the competition in the marketplace. The sport organizations links to the community and customers is often a key factor in developing new ideas. Some sport organizations are more innovation orientated, which has an impact on the number of new ventures that are created. Other sport organizations are changing to have more willingness to develop innovations as a response to market needs.

There are old and new forms of innovation affecting sport organizations. The old forms represent past initiatives that were aiming to change the sport industry and are still under development. The new forms involve futuristic ideas that are radically different to current thinking. Both types of innovations are motivated by the objectives to transform the current products or processes in existence. These innovations offer a useful solution to problems or gaps in the marketplace that are of interest for the sports industry.

The term sport entrepreneurship is a matter of both fitness and innovation in terms of its applicability to the marketplace. There is a need to reinforce the need for sport entrepreneurship by offering a multidisciplinary approach to its development. This is the result of connections with sport and entrepreneurship being observed in business, management and the social sciences. The entrepreneurship part of sport entrepreneurship has gained importance as a result of changing technology trends. Part of the entrepreneurship involves the creativity and creation of business ventures in sport. Organizations involved in sport need to lead the change and incorporate more entrepreneurship in order to bring about strategic change. Any improvements to the sport sector can bring about social and technological advances in other fields.

Technology disruption can involve a number of processes, which is why it is important to care about the innovation steps needed to increase performance. More specifically, the innovation needs to incorporate a plan about the objectives from the sport entrepreneurship. This includes improving functionality whilst incorporating new procedures that maintain existing standards. Despite the prominence of entrepreneurship in the global economy, there are very few studies linking entrepreneurship to sport. This is despite there being a close relationship between sport and entrepreneurship that is changing the boundaries between both fields. Most of the traditional sport literature has been shaped on organizational behavior and management aspects. The new view in entrepreneurship is part of the process as its strategic focus has an impact on sport. Thus, the sport entrepreneurship process is determined by more than innovation and organizational behavior but the complex interaction in the environment. Sport entrepreneurship relies on the market structure of the industry to bring about change. The market characteristics will determine the efficiency of the sport entrepreneurship. This is due to the process of entrepreneurship being complementary and dependent to sport.

7.2.6 Innovation Creation Process

A people-centered focus to the innovation creation process in sport is useful to obtain better results. The innovation processes in sport need to be aligned to the rest of an organizations strategy. This means incorporating the already known innovation processes to extend the boundaries of the sport organization. Sport entrepreneurship can take place in a variety of contexts but normally requires cross-sectoral collaboration with stakeholders working together on a project. This means the entrepreneurship will evolve and contribute to achieving the common goals of a sport organization.

There needs to be the appropriate information in order to sustain the sport entrepreneurship. This can come from different stakeholders including customers, suppliers and sport research institutes. Information from internal sources of the organization is helpful in linking the innovation to current management practices. Then market sources of information in terms of competitiveness can help further the innovation process. In addition, research from public and private institutions is often useful to innovation occurring in sport. These different sources of information need to be combined to see what the most productive is in order to strengthen the idea. The most influential source of information is how the market responds to the innovation. This will influence the future innovation capabilities of sport organizations.

A sport organizations decision to orientate towards entrepreneurship is closely linked to their environment. This means the customers, competitors and stakeholders of a sport organization contributes to the entrepreneurship process. For an innovation in sport to progress it needs to have the appropriate information that leads to a solution or market need. This involves creating shared value by facilitating the orientation towards innovation.

Sport organizations that try to maintain their competitive position need to focus on entrepreneurship. It can be expected that different types of innovation will have an impact on the development of sport entrepreneurship. This means it might be useful to elucidate the innovation process when a sport organization wants to experiment with current offerings. Sport organizations can improve their firm's knowledge by collaborating with immediate clients and suppliers. This helps improve a sport organizations skills in harnessing their entrepreneurial capacity.

Most sport organizations have often an unprecedented reach in the global market to contribute to entrepreneurship. The market constraints of geography and distance have decreased due to the internet, which has increased the market potential for sports entrepreneurship. The process of entrepreneurship in sport is interactive and requires close collaboration amongst stakeholders. Well aware of the importance of entrepreneurship, sport organizations are attaching more weight to innovation and creativity. For instance, the National Football League has pioneered interactive technology on players uniforms. There is also pressure on sport organizations to be entrepreneurial in their quest to be the best.

There is a strong sentiment amongst sport organizations that entrepreneurship requires cross-sector collaboration. Entrepreneurship can speed up the reforms of sport institutions to make them more proactive and engaged members of a community. Sport organizations need to be provided with the opportunities relating to their participation in entrepreneurship. The growth of the global sport industry means the adoption of more entrepreneurial policies. This means clarifying the entrepreneurship approaches organizations should take in terms of how they will maintain their global competitiveness.

7.2.7 Sport Industry Processes

The sport industry has experience in changing and it is expected that it will become more entrepreneurial in the future. Entrepreneurship will play a crucial role in sustaining the development of the sport industry. Research carried out in sport will contribute to the entrepreneurship in the industry. Sport organizations need to develop a more flexible approach in response to entrepreneurship. Therefore, the ability of sport organizations to be entrepreneurial depends on their approaches and economic activity. Most sport organizations are optimistic about the future of their industry. The quest for sport entrepreneurship and attempts to advance technology needs to tackle the future needs of the marketplace. This involves coordinating the proper way to engage in sport entrepreneurship.

Most sport organizations provide encouragement to improve their business practices. Politicians often focus on sport initiatives as a way to engage with the community. This has led to interest about how sport can be used for policy objectives. Despite the interest in sport there is little debate about how entrepreneurship generates successful sport products and processes. It has been noted that sport management research has tended to ignore the role of entrepreneurship and how it impacts the sport sector. After neglecting the entrepreneurship field research on sport entrepreneurship is beginning to expand. The simplest kind of entrepreneurship in sport is the creation of new products or services.

Sport entrepreneurs produce innovation, which underpins the economic growth of the industry. According to this perspective, a sports entrepreneur is the one that develops an idea and puts it into the business world. This means sport entrepreneurship is a creative act that enables the development of a new idea. The idea behind sports entrepreneurship is that an idea adds value to society. This means capturing an opportunity through creating a unique product or service that changes the current state of the market. This involves a dynamic process and requires the entrepreneurial capacity to see it come to fruition in the market.

The appropriate infrastructure is required in order to exploit the change in the marketplace. There is considerable overlap between sport and entrepreneurship as both tend to focus on competitiveness. Thus, the objective of sport and entrepreneurship is to address market needs in a successful manner. The sport world has a profound influence on entrepreneurship in other sectors. Sport is often the place where ideas are tested and commercialized. The sporting culture influences how things are done and the way innovation is implemented in the market. Thus, the norms and values in sport such as equality and fairness are reflected in entrepreneurship. Many believe sport has a emotional attachment to many people that necessitates a different kind of approach to entrepreneurship. The procedures to create sport entrepreneurship are shaped by the values of an organization.

In order to facilitate the process of entrepreneurship in a sport organization there needs to be proper management to measure and monitor its success. This is important as organizations change and there needs to be a focus on the way the sport idea is progressing. Sport entrepreneurship needs to be integrated into the management structure of an organization. This can involve an informal system that still has managers controlling the process but enabling a flexible approach. There needs to be persistence by sport entrepreneurs in ensuring they have the necessary resources in order to make improvements. The style of the managers involved in the entrepreneurship needs to have the right skills in order to learn from successes and failures. This means developing an appropriate strategy to stimulate sports entrepreneurship in organizations. Strategy can involve planning about how to address the human, financial, social and technological issues associated with the sports entrepreneurship. This involves focusing on the future objectives of the sport entrepreneur to be congruent with anticipated change in the marketplace.

Given the synergies between sport and entrepreneurship the strategy should maintain existing strategies whilst progressing on future needs. Thus, meeting the requirements of customers whilst developing a feasible strategy for the entrepreneurship is important. The capacity to exploit knowledge through entrepreneurship is important in sport organizations. This helps to accumulate information about how to have an effective execution of entrepreneurship in the market. A supportive management style will help make entrepreneurship a reality for sports organizations. Often people in the sports environment are the most important asset in ensuring the success of the entrepreneurship. This can include people who have a flair for creativity and are keen to exploit change. These people need to take a conscientious effort to implement the sport entrepreneurship by obtaining the right mix of people needed to progress it into the market.

7.2.8 Sport Organizations

Sport organizations need to have the ability to convert ideas into commercially viable innovations. This involves the integration of market knowledge into effective ideas that involve identifying opportunities. Sport organizations that have a proactive attitude are able to create an environment that fosters entrepreneurship. This includes absorbing information from the market about the quality and commercial value of the innovation. To do this it requires an incentive structure for entrepreneurial behaviors. Some sport organizations need to be culturally conditioned to engage in entrepreneurial behavior. This means not all sport organizations will be able to implement innovations that are representative of market demands.

Entrepreneurship is vital to the success of sport organizations in today's rapidly changing environment. Systematic efforts are needed to focus on entrepreneurship in sport organizations. This means entrepreneurship should be regarded as an ongoing practice in sport. Often sport ventures are developed as a way to capture more marketshare or enter new market segments. Due to emerging new technologies, some sport ventures are established as a way to manage the growing business. This is then scaled into bigger sport ventures depending on the success and market demand. In order for sport ventures to succeed they need to be sustainable in the long term. This can mean sport ventures internationalizing as a way to harvest the successful business ideas.

More sport organizations have a commitment to being entrepreneurial in their businesses. This disposition to entrepreneurship encourages an understanding of the competitive market environment as to how sport is changing. Sport business researchers have been largely interested in the role of health, fitness and leisure in the creation of new businesses. The correlation between sport and entrepreneurship varies across geographical and industry contexts. In the highly competitive sport environment, knowledge helps determine whether sport entrepreneurs can recognize opportunities.

Desbordes (2001: 124) states that sport products are viewed as "technologically complex because it requires varied and complementary competencies (for example in such areas as chemicals, mechanics, textiles, metallurgy)". Sport organizations can undergo a process of renewal that enables the development of specific capacities. Entrepreneurial activities are necessary for sport organizations to progress and go international. Sport entrepreneurs focus on novel ways they can add products or services to the industry. This means persevering after setbacks that might affect the development of a business. To do this sport entrepreneurs need to have a degree of creativity in influencing how they implement new business ideas. This can involve using their human relations skills to communicate knowledge about sport ideas.

The desire to be an entrepreneur means that there is a desire for initiative. Thus, recognizing the need for achievement is a key feature of sport entrepreneurs. Many sport entrepreneurs focus on strategic practices in terms of how their business venture can progress beyond the conception stage. However, not all sport organizations are entrepreneurial due to the willingness to remain the same and sell rather than innovate new products or services. There are different types of entrepreneurial sport ventures that range from introducing new goods, alternative methods of production, opening new markets, having different courses of supply and industrial reorganization.

7.3   Conclusion

There has been an ignorance of the entrepreneurship literature on sport due to the focus on psychology and other disciplines. Thus, entrepreneurship needs further exploration in a sport context in order to develop a research agenda. This chapter piques the interest in how sport is utilizing entrepreneurship for competitive reasons by focusing on the process of entrepreneurship. Thus, this chapter will fuel further interest in sport entrepreneurship by stressing the processual elements important to overall performance.

References

Borgers, J., Breedveld, K., Tiessen-Raaphorst, A., Thibaut, E., Vandermeerschen, H., Vos, S., & Scheerder, J. (2016). A study on the frequency of participation and time spent on sport in different organisational settings. *European Sport Management Quarterly, 16*(5), 635–654.

Comeaux, E. (2013). Rethinking academic reform and encouraging organizational innovation: Implications for stakeholder management in college sports. *Innovation Higher Education, 38*, 281–293.

Desbordes, M. (2001). Innovation management in the sports industry: Lessons from the Salomon case. *European Sport Management Quarterly, 1*(2), 124–149.

Haugh, H. (2005). A research agenda for social entrepreneurship. *Social Enterprise Journal, 1*(1), 1–12.

Madrigal, R. (2000). The influence of social alliances with sports teams on intentions to purchase corporate sponsors products. *Journal of Advertising, 29*(4), 13–24.

Morrison, A. (2000). Entrepreneurship: What triggers it? *International Journal of Entrepreneurial Behavior & Research, 6*(2), 59–71.

Pehkonen, S., & Ikonen, H. M. (2016). Too good to be a sport? Why dog agility struggles in gaining recognition as a sport. *International Review for the Sociology of Sport.* https://doi.org/10.1177/1012690216679834

Pinch, S., & Henry, N. (1999). Discursive aspects of technological innovation: The case of the British motor sport industry. *Environment and Planning A, 31*, 665–682.

Provasnek, A. K., Schmid, E., Geissler, B., & Steiner, G. (2017). Sustainable corporate entrepreneurship: Performance and strategies toward innovation. *Business Strategy and the Environment, 26*(4), 521–535.

Spaaij, R., & Westerbeek, H. (2010). Sport business and social capital: A contradiction in terms? *Sport in Society, 13*(9), 1356–1373.

Zhao, F. (2005). Exploring the synergy between entrepreneurship and innovation. *International Journal of Entrepreneurial Behavior & Research, 11*(1), 25–41.

Ethics and Sport Entrepreneurship

8

8.1 Introduction

Sport is part of the social fabric of society and plays an important role in fostering ethical behavior. This is evident in Austin (2017: 2) stating that there are "prominent moral failings that exist in and around sport". Ethics is an important issue in sport and is constantly changing due to technological advances. The ethics of sport changes with new knowledge developed about appropriate codes of conduct. However, ethics is a diverse and debatable topic that needs to be understood according to type of sport, cultural environment and existence of social problems. Hervieux and Voltan (2016: 3) define social problems as "socially constructed and based on conditions and conduct deemed troublesome by individuals and groups". In sport there are social problems that create ethical issues, which depend on the environmental context.

The ethics of sport refers to the ways of regulating behaviours and expected conduct in games involving physical or mental activity. Sport ethics is a distinctive discipline that plays an important role in influencing other sport fields and is entrepreneurial in three main ways. Firstly, through deliberate action about the need for change and innovative thinking about the role of ethics in sport. This means that there can be a purposive approach to integrating entrepreneurship in sport ethics to provide a way to understand future behavior. This involves looking at actions sport entities are taking in terms of being more proactive about future ethics issues. In addition, it helps provide a sense of vision about the role ethics plays in the development of sport. Secondly, there are unplanned or accidental forms of entrepreneurship in sport ethics. This occurs when inadvertently there are changes required in the understanding of ethics in sport due to technology advances. As technology is altering quickly there needs to be societal changes about ethics. This means often sport ethics is reactive instead of proactive about decisions they make in terms of regulations. Thirdly, there are evolutionary forms of entrepreneurship in sport ethics. This means that there are developments about people's perceptions of sport ethics in terms of how it is embedded in society. Some beliefs about ethics in sport are traditional and culturally based that take time to change. However, other values are tied to the way sport is seen in society.

There is assumption that socially motivated types of sport such as community and non-profit are ethically sound. This is often not the case due to the strategies and politics behind the offering of sport to the public. The question at the heart of the intersection between sport ethics and entrepreneurship is how are sport ethics evolving based on entrepreneurship? In this chapter I argue that ethics in sport is fundamentally entrepreneurial. The goal of this chapter is to bring entrepreneurship into the sports ethics literature. Thus, in this chapter I focus on sport ethics from an entrepreneurship perspective and anticipate this field will develop in the future. In this chapter there is an overview of sport ethics that then is linked to entrepreneurship. The chapter begins by providing a summary of key sport ethics issues and doing so opens the field up to an integration of entrepreneurship perspectives. I hope that this chapter is only the beginning of an ongoing discussion about entrepreneurship and sport ethics thereby fostering more work on the intersection of sport ethics and entrepreneurship. In this chapter, I go beyond just looking at sport ethics and entrepreneurship as disparate fields but by providing a more integrated approach into how they affect each other. The chapter ends by presenting some suggestions about future directions concerning entrepreneurship and sport ethics.

8.2   Ethics

Ethics is a controversial topic as its definition changes according to context. Some people view ethics as a minor issue due to the need to outperform competitors at any cost in sport. This leads to ethical misconduct viewed as mistakes rather than conscious action. In addition, unethical action can be viewed as necessary for the teams benefit. The way ethics is perceived is constantly changing and is a fluid concept. There are challenges in managing ethics in sport due to the reliance on self-reporting and peer pressure. Whilst some unethical behavior such as cheating or doping can be tested it can depend on the timing and availability of regulators to enforce it. This was evident with Lance Armstrong the multiple winner of the Tour de France bike race who constantly kept hidden his unethical behavior. There was also discussion with Lance Armstrong how other cyclists were doing the same thing so the question became whether it was really cheating. The controversy of Lance Armstrong meant there were unethical judgments on his previous performances that might have been ethically sound but nonetheless were perceived as cheating. This leads to it being difficult to evaluate ethics in sport and the ramifications of unethical conduct.

The demands of high performance sport and electronic participation in sport require a new way of understanding ethical behavior. There are different reasons in sport why people adhere to certain obligations and this depends on the type of sport under investigation. Shogun and Ford (2000: 52) states in sport "participants may abide by rules because coerced, to maintain an image as a 'good' competitor, for experience, or because of a desire to honour a perceived agreement with competitors". The reasons for ethical conduct link to the notion of sport being an activity that favours fairness in competition. The fairness depends on the type of sport in terms of whether it is regulated or unregulated. In regulated sports there are rules of the game that are needed and help compare performance. This includes tacit or unwritten rules about appropriate behavior in sport. Thus, natural competition ensures the best person or team wins in sport. Unregulated sport also has moral obligations due to the informal nature of the competition. This can also include competition with oneself rather than others in sport. In addition, there are unethical values found in sport that are part of the culture. This includes playing against unequal opponents when the chance of having a fair game is low. This creates moral dilemmas in sport, which are an important element of ethical management practices.

8.3 Ethics and Sport Entrepreneurship

There needs to be a more fluid understanding about the interaction of entrepreneurship and sport ethics as they have practical implications. This is the result of there being pressing issues that need to be discussed in terms of entrepreneurship and sport ethics that will influence the future scholarship concerning sport entrepreneurship. It is surprising that little research has connected entrepreneurship to sport ethics, since it influences change in the sport industry. Entrepreneurship in the forms of new businesses are featured prominently in discussions around sport ethics. However, there is a gap in the sport literature in combining ethics issues to entrepreneurship.

Chell et al. (2016: 623) states "entrepreneurship has been bedeviled with myths". These myths impact ethical issues in entrepreneurship as there are assumptions made that often might not be relevant to current society. Entrepreneurship in sport ethics involves considering new types and reasons of behavior based on emerging trends. Whilst research might consider entrepreneurship as a newcomer to the field of sport ethics, it has been an important influencer of activity. Ethics in a way is fundamentally about change, which is at the core of entrepreneurships research. Moreover, the expansion in entrepreneurship research has coincided with an increase in sport ethics studies but they have typically been seen as disparate and unrelated fields. There is more sport policy concerning ethics and initiatives around diversity and gender equality in sport.

Sport entrepreneurship has not received much academic attention until only recently. Sports that are unregulated often have rogue behavior and encourage unethical conduct. Sport has been commended for ignoring race and religion in the pursuit of a fairer playing field but there is still some degree of discrimination in the form of unethical conduct. This means that some sports particularly adventure sports pride themselves on their risk taking activity and propensity to push boundaries. For this reason, whilst adventure sports have become more regulated there is still the perception that unethical behavior is part of the sport. This means that some sports are open avenues to unethical conduct due to their link to performance. Thus, a distinguishing feature of entrepreneurship is the ability to integrate innovativeness in the sport context. Russell and Faulkner (2004) discuss how entrepreneurship is a form of chaos in the lifestyle of certain industries. This means that the sport industry utilizes entrepreneurship as a way to link risky activity to the pursuit of business ventures. Risk often involves ethical questions about the appropriate form of behavior given the circumstances.

To date, there has been a lack of research about sport ethics and entrepreneurship, which implies there is an ample opportunity for more research on this topic. It is interesting to see whether there are noticeable differences between sport entrepreneurs and other types of entrepreneurs in terms of their ethical behavior. There might be a need to stimulate more ethical conduct amongst sport entrepreneurs. Thus by integrating an entrepreneurial perspective into sport ethics it can yield a more integrated understanding of the field. This will help support more ethical business conduct amongst sport entrepreneurs.

Entrepreneurs are a core component of the sport industry. The future of the sport industry is based on ethical conduct so it is important to understand the behaviours of entrepreneurs. Sport entrepreneurship is a distinctive field of entrepreneurship that demands a special approach to ethics. Although there has been research on ethics and sport, little research has focused on entrepreneurship. Entrepreneurship involves behavior concerning business activity. Thus, the process of entrepreneurship involves interpreting the environment and its effects on individuals and society. Currently ethics in sport is focused on the management literature with little linkage to entrepreneurship. This has inhibited a more holistic understanding of the role entrepreneurship plays in sport ethics.

Edgar (2013: 1) states that sport provides a way "metaphysical and normative problems are articulated". This is due to sport being part of the culture and having an impact on society conditions. Sport has typically been governed by rules and physical activity although some sports instead utilize mental fitness (Edgar 2013). The sport industry has a large degree of economic and social power that means it should have ethical responsibilities. In addition, due to its impact on communities it has a moral duty to ensure ethical conduct. This is important as ethics involves consideration about business strategy and decisions making in sport.

Often sport is conducted through actions that are interpreted by players. This means that rather than verbal communication the emphasis in sport is on physical action. The actual playing of sport involves non-verbal communication but the commentary is mostly verbally-based. Edgar (2013: 8) states that sport "takes the materials, ideas and fundamental experiences of our cultural existence, and plays with them". This means that sport is a cultural aspect that involves unwritten rules that are based on the cultural context of the environment.

There needs to be new interpretations of sport ethics based on changing technology and needs of society. This means entrepreneurship can provide a way to revitalize sports ethics to make it more progressive. Sport organizations need to use more entrepreneurial approaches in their dealings with sport ethics. A way to do this is to include more proactive strategies rather than have a passive stance towards ethics. This can include anticipating trends and issues in sport that will cause ethical dilemmas.

Sport is viewed as pure when there is a no artificial interference from other sources. At the heart of ethics in sport is the role of equal opportunities. Konig (1995: 249) defines equal opportunities as "the equal position of both athletes before the competition with the same changes to win, despite the intended equality after the competition brought about by the code of victory/defeat". These equal opportunities have been hampered by unethical conduct in sport such as cheating and doping. The forms of unethical conduct can be formal and informal depending on the circumstances. Formal ethical violations include match tampering by officials or umpires whilst informal include the taking of banned substances. Performance improvement is the aim of most unethical conduct and this is influenced by technological innovation. Thus, sport regulators need to take an entrepreneurship approach in terms of how they handle unethical conduct. However, it can be hard to evaluate ethics in sport due to constant change from new medical and scientific advancements.

As sport management scholars have started to incorporate more ethics into their research, they have in turn contributed to an improved understanding of the role of sport in society. The field of sport ethics has experienced significant growth that has coincided with more general interest about ethical issues such as corporate social responsibility and environmental management. This has led to more research on sport ethics focusing on initiatives around sustainability that today are more strategically important for sport organizations. As part of the increased interest in business ethics there are some promising new research areas linking it to entrepreneurship. Whilst past research looked at sport ethics, business and entrepreneurship as separate research areas, this chapter will propose combining theme for future enquiry. This includes using entrepreneurial thinking to maximize the potential of sport ethics in terms of its relevance for business. In addition, it acknowledges that sport can be used as a strategic vehicle to implement better business ethics principles. Thereby, enabling a closer sport management link between ethics and entrepreneurship that can contribute to academic discourse.

The impact of entrepreneurship in sport management in terms of the ethical issues is brings has received scant scholarly attention. New technology and less reliance on public funding in sport have meant that sport organizations are under more pressure to be competitive. This is evident in the limited time and resources available to sport organizations to come up with new ideas. Many areas of a sport organization concern ethics from sponsorship of sport stadiums to the use of taxpayer money. Thus, the combination of both public and private finance in sport gives rise to a number of ethical challenges. Some areas of sport particularly non-profit organizations face scrutiny about how to grow in an ethical manner.

Sometimes there are forced ethics measures and implications of ethics in sport due to regulations. This enables sport organizations to navigate ethics by adjusting their management practices. Thus, ethics in sport involves individuals questioning its relevance in contemporary society. Sport ethics is a result of the morals and expected behavior required in society. In times of economic uncertainty the role of ethics in sport is exacerbated due to financial concerns. The austerity measures caused by the global financial crisis of 2008 are still evident in the ethical guidelines of sport organizations (Parnell et al. 2017).

Dey and Steyaert (2016: 627) states "ethics has had a dubious career in the domain of entrepreneurship studies". This is due to the perception by many of entrepreneurship as being unethical as it involves risk taking. However, entrepreneurship can and should be ethical as it relates to business practices. There has been an increase in studies linking entrepreneurship to ethics due to the need for business to behave in a socially responsible manner. Entrepreneurship often involves value creation and enables better work prospects. For this reason, sub-fields of entrepreneurship such as social and women's entrepreneurship tend to emphasise more ethics issues. Social entrepreneurship combines both non-profit and profit objectives in a business endeavour. Hence, there is an overt linkage with ethics in social entrepreneurship due to the acknowledgement of the need to help disadvantaged members of society.

Increasingly business is marketing its social initiatives in activities as a way to highlight their social role. This helps with businesses that need to report their social indicators to be part of industry groups. There are also negative connotations between entrepreneurship and ethics that are evident particularly in public policy reports. This has meant ethics has been viewed skeptically in entrepreneurship studies due to the need for business to focus on financial gain at the expense of social needs (Dey and Steyaert 2016). When a business starts a new venture there is often a power play involved particularly with large businesses. This means that large businesses or multinationals can have more power in the market due to their existing relationships. In emerging and developing economies there has been some criticism of the ethical practices of large businesses in terms of entrepreneurship. This is due to many large businesses being from developed countries and having a different culture. This creates ethical issues in terms of the businesses they are developing in countries outside their home market. Part of this perception is subjective as there are different connotations on what is considered moral behavior. Entrepreneurship has been typically about business development that involves change, which can be viewed negatively. Often government policy or help is needed in entrepreneurial business ventures that create ethics issues when bribery is involved. Moreover, the lobbying of government officials for support on business ventures is viewed by some as being unethical.

Ethics involves behavior that can be subjective and influenced by environmental constraints. In the sport context ethics is practiced through the actions of athletes, coaches and managers. This involves action that when conducted in a creative and proactive way exhibits signs of entrepreneurial leadership. Part of the process of ethics involves criticizing or reviewing past behavior as a way to conduct better actions in the future. Existing relationships in sport need to be managed in terms of ethical behavior as the actions of others can have flow on effects.

There is a team structure evident in many sports, which means the ethical conduct of one person will affect others. The knowledge a person has about events or circumstances influences their ethical behavior. There is debate about the parameters of ethical conduct in sport due to differences in opinion about what constitutes ethics. The foundations of sport are built around ethics but there is a continuum of good to bad ethical practices. Traditionally most of the ethics violations in sport occurred at the individual level but they can also occur at the team level. This occurred with the

New England Patriots who were accused of spying on the field plays of another football team. In their case the use of cameras to record the plays of another football team was considered unethical. However, the response from the National Football League to this conduct was considered by some as not being hard enough given the impact of the conduct on the performance of the team. This means that it is often hard to penalize unethical conduct in sport as there is some uncertainty about the effects it has on performance.

There are many moral issues associated with ethics in sport. Recently Colin Kaepernik in the National Football League knelt during the playing of the American anthem in protest of racism in sport. This action was copied by others in different sports as a form of protect against racial conduct both in sport but also non sport activities. There has been some debate about the use of sport to protest against racism, gender inequality and other issues. In addition, the use of sport to market products such as alcohol and gambling has been raised as an ethical issue by some sport policy analysts. This is due to the role sport has in people's lives especially young people who may be more susceptible to marketing campaigns. In the past cigarette advertising was used extensively in sport including through sponsorship agreements and billboard advertising. Now cigarette advertising in banned in many sports where it was previously a source of revenue including cricket events. Benson and Hedges a cigarette company previously sponsored cricket events in Australia but this has since ceased. Some sports utilized anti-smoking campaigns sponsored by the government in their advertising. An example is the Quit campaign by the Victorian government in Australia to encourage people to stop smoking by promoting it at the Bells beach surfing context. In the National Football League there has also been the use of athletes to provide anti-violence towards women campaigns. As athletes are often viewed highly in society their endorsements about certain practices can have a big effect.

Recognition about entrepreneurial ethical behavior in sport has emerged belatedly in the academic literature. The differing kinds of ethical conduct in sport are evident in the Olympics, which promotes the event as bring together different types of sport with international participation. The positive impacts are in terms of promoting sport as a vehicle for international peace and collaboration but there are negative side effects from the politics involved in hosting the event. The Rio de Janeiro Olympics of 2016 enabled more attention placed on Brazil but the side effects included the displacement of communities to make way for the building of new stadiums.

Sport organizations vary in how much they emphasise ethics, which is considered as appropriate behavior given moral and societal duties. Some sport organizations such as community or non-profit are focused almost exclusively on ethical ways to conduct sport. This is the result of ethics being a byproduct of sport and an easy way to encourage a more open and inclusive society. Sport is seen by some as a language or form of communication. This means that conduct in sport will be viewed as a way to influence positively other parts of society. Sport entrepreneurs apply ethical principles to many of the challenges they face in the marketplace. Entrepreneurial ethics is a way sport can adapt to the market but also create social value.

Sport when it is ethically managed has the potential to contribute to a more harmonious society. Increasing attention is directed towards ethics in sport and its importance in affecting other parts of society. It has been emphasized that the appraising of ethical guidelines in sport can be difficult due to different conceptualizations of what is ethical conduct. This means that ethics is inherently entrepreneurial due to its changing nature and role in sport. Ethical conduct is required in sport because rules and guidelines must be followed as part of fair play. The backdrop of competition in sport, encompassing a gap between performing and non-performing clubs has implications for entrepreneurial ethics. There are often cultural conditions that affect the ability of some sport teams to behave ethically. The intention of entrepreneurial ethics is to assist sport clubs and athletes perform within guidelines. Thus, the aim is to bestow sport clubs with the ability to utilize ethics in a positive way.

Sport practitioners need to value ethics due to the potential effects it can have on athlete and team moral. Some sports are more prone to ethical questions particularly those concerning animals. Horse racing is amongst the most popular sports but some animal rights activists suggest that it includes unethical conduct due to the treatment of animals. This is reflected in racehorses being put down after their competitive career has finished. Another sport often highlighted by animal rights activists is greyhound racing. This is due to the dogs being taught to race and being breed particularly for this reason. Illegal dog fighting is a related sport that has been a source of controversy. However, some sports have changed from being unethical and radical to mainstream sports. This is evident in the Ultimate Fight Championships with its use of mixed martial arts being amongst the highest worldwide growth sports.This chapter can be a starting point for further discussion on entrepreneurial sport ethics.

Sport entrepreneurs come up with new ideas to issues in sport that are different to current practices. This is due to sport playing a key role in communities and the use of ethics can bring about a better overall result. Sport entrepreneurs are active at the management level by directing ethical objectives. This enables change to occur through entrepreneurial action that incorporates an ethical stance. The impact of ethics on sport management is a well recognized stream of research. The search for entrepreneurial ways to respond to ethical concerns in sport is less known but an important source of competitive advantage.

Sport is considered as an important way to encourage social cohesion through healthy activities that encourage wellbeing. Entrepreneurship captures many of the change and forward thinking outlook needed in sport ethics. People are attracted to sport due to the passion and connection they feel to the game and athletes. Sport is considered as wholesome as it is marketed in that way. However, the glamour and money involved in sport makes it subject to unethical behavior.

The culture of sport has distinct behaviours that are in accordance with entrepreneurship such as aggressiveness and risk taking behavior. This had led to sport organizations needing to participate in ethical conduct in a way that reflects their cultural conditions. In addition, ethics is reflected in the way sports people behave and interact with the community. This means the practice of ethics is important to sports entrepreneurship as it is a component of the entrepreneurial ecosystem.

There are moral dilemmas faced by sport organizations based on their position in society. Often government authorities engage with both public and private sporting bodies in order to understand the impact of moral transgressions. Despite this cross-partnership collaboration sport ethics is a vexed question and still under studied. For sport entrepreneurs, the ethics issue remains problematic due to uncertain aspects about its implications. This is noted by sport organizations perceiving ethics to not be critical to the overall functioning of their team.

Scholarship related to sport ethics has been dominated by medical and technology issues. This is not surprising given the amount of money spent on new sports products and services. This logic is based on the increasingly technological sophisticated sport services that are linked to the internet. For many years there has been considerable interest about the way artificial intelligence will change sport and this is reflected in ethics issues. From the perspective of sport organizations less attention has been placed on entrepreneurship. This is interesting as sport is inherently entrepreneurial and there is much to be studied about ethics. Entrepreneurs as practitioners strive to have a place in the market by developing new ideas that are likely to have successful outcomes. Shilbury et al. (2008: 217) conceptualizes sport development as being "about participation and promoting the opportunities and benefits of participation". People experience sport in different ways depending on their interests in being a participant or observer. Sport can foster exchange of knowledge and information amongst stakeholders that can lead to innovation. Often the development of regions and states is derived from sport related activities. Schulenkorf (2017: 243) states "sport is a conduit to achieving wider development outcomes rather than an end in itself".

Given the buzz around entrepreneurship in the economy, it seems fair to say that the field of sport entrepreneurship will continue to experience significant growth. In order to harness existing knowledge in sport there needs to be more appreciation of how entrepreneurship can contribute to the development of the field. Over time, entrepreneurship in sport will be more strategically planned as a way to engage in long term development. In the past, entrepreneurship was considered as an ad-ho or by-product of sport. In the future more notice of how entrepreneurship occurs in sport will be known.

There are different philosophies in sport that effect ethics. For some competition means winning at any costs including through cheating or immoral activity. The responsibility is on the referees or regulators to catch the unethical conduct rather than the perpetrators. This means there is some ambiguity when ethics is interpreted differently by people. An example is the football inflation rate tampering case by the New England Patriots, who deliberately under-inflated footballs in order to give their team an advantage in the game. Tom Brady the quarterback from the New England Patriots was suspended for a number of games but ultimately his team won the Super Bowl and was named the most valuable player in the game. Hence, the unethical behavior seemed to have a positive effect, which further encourages others to engage in the same kind of conduct.

Gamesmanship is a term used in sport that has ethical implications depending on the context and extent of the behavior. For some, sport is about politics and to win there needs to be some manipulation of conduct for the aim of winning. This is evident in faking an injury that was popular in football before referees started to penalize players who seemed to be over emphasizing their injury. There is now more ability through replay technology to see whether a player has actually been injured. In addition, there are name calling in sport as part of the psychological warfare that goes on in sport. This has been considered as part of the game but recently there has been a backlash against this kind of conduct especially when it concerns gender or race. In the Australian Football League an infamous incident was in 1993 when St Kilda player Nicky Winmar lifted his jumper during a game to point to his Aboriginal skin in response to racial abuse from the crowd at a game. This incident resulted in the AFL creating an anti-racist policy that tried to educate and inform players and fans that racism was not tolerated in the sport. The AFL has also tried to educate people about homophobia and transphobia by starting pride games that encourage equal equality.

There are ethical issues associated with the environmental impact of sport events. This stems from the crowing and amount of people coming to a place to see a sport event. Often sport events in natural environments such as those in parks or in the ocean cause disruption to the existing animal and plant life. This congestion can have detrimental long term effects to an area so the sport events need to be managed more sustainably. Local communities have responded to these environmental concerns by tying to be more involved in the sport event. Despite the negative environmental effects there can also be positive effects in terms of more media and attention placed on an area. This helps a region gain funding and sponsorship from their association with a sport. An example is World Surfing Reserves, which has named specific surfing spots as places that need special environmental protection. Bells Beach Surfing Reserve located 1 h from Melbourne has a national park next to the beach and limited tourism development. This is in contrast to the Gold Coast in Queensland that has emphasized tourism development through skyscrapers and large amounts of apartment buildings. Thus, sports events have a destination image that needs to be managed in the appropriate manner.

The destination of some sport events such as yacht racing need to take place in a big area but others is limited to stadiums or smaller spaces. This has caused some security issues associated with the number of people able to attend a sports event. Whilst some see sport as a vehicle for change and argue everyone should have access to it there can be restrictions based on the amount of financial resources required to play or watch the sport. For example, sports such as tennis and golf are viewed as elitist sports and this represents an ethics issue as not all segments of society can play the sport. Thus, there needs to be an integration of commercial goals and social transformation in the hosting of sport events.

The novelty of sport means there are specific qualities it has that impact on the way opportunities are pursued. The process of sports entrepreneurship involves change through the innovative use of resources. There is entrepreneurial behavior in sport that enables continued innovation in existing contexts but also the establishment of new business opportunities. The capacity of sport organizations to engage in risk depends on how they recognize opportunities. Sport entrepreneurship involves entrepreneurial activity within the sports context. Increasing studies on sport are acknowledging that entrepreneurship is a key contributor to the creation of new opportunities. The development of sport is dependent on exploiting opportunities. Entrepreneurship has outcomes for the way sport is delivered and for its development. There is a paucity of research on the way entrepreneurial ethics are conducted in both the public and private sport sector. One of the biggest challenges for sport organizations is to find new opportunities that can enhance their market position. Sport has substantial social and economic value and is recognized as a key component of communities. Many regions emphasise sport as being part of the social fabric in enabling a community spirit to develop. Sport can provide a way for groups of people to come together and connect.

8.4 Looking Ahead

The sport context provides a range of contexts for investigating the role of entrepreneurship and ethics. The sport sector plays a key role in integrating new technology and medical breakthroughs that have ethical dilemmas. Therefore, sport leaders play a crucial role in making sure ethical guidelines are adhered to but also respect emerging technologies. The increase in sport technology innovation alongside increased ethical responsibility of sport organizations makes it more important for firms in sport ethics. The viability of sport organizations refers to their need to act ethical but also to innovate. Sport organizations need to develop strategies to attract innovation whilst safeguarding ethical principles. Previous research has focused on the role of sport ethics but has not linked it to entrepreneurship as there are challenges of sport ethics in keeping up to date with emerging technology. This has often resulted in ineffective ethics policies that resulted in bad governance practices. As government funding to sport changes there is a need for more independent funding of sport ventures that brings with it ethical challenges. To overcome ethics issues sport organizations need to decrease their financial dependence on public institutions and incorporate more entrepreneurial funding.

I suggest that entrepreneurship can provide opportunities for sport organizations to keep up to date with emerging technology in an ethical manner. Academics can provide some suggestions about the use of entrepreneurial ethics in other sectors that can then be applied to sport. Therefore, entrepreneurial ethics utilized in sport can enable the development of research partnerships between academic and practice. Given the interest in sports developing ethical guidelines in a new way may help benefit other sectors of the economy. Sport organizations need to respond to the ethical issues they are facing and develop new mechanisms to cope with change. This will have an impact to the sport industry but also related sectors. This chapter offers an entrepreneurial perspective to sport ethics. I hope the impact of sport ethics and entrepreneurship will further stimulate research. The goal of this chapter was to fuel interest in the need for a more entrepreneurial approach to sport ethics.

Sport entrepreneurship is a newly developed research field that is rapidly gaining acceptance in both the sport management and entrepreneurship disciplines. In the future ethics and sport entrepreneurship will continue to gain prominence in the academic literature. Entrepreneurship is one of the fastest growing fields of business so it is natural to assume sport entrepreneurship will increase in prominence. It can be expected that the role of ethics in sport entrepreneurship will be deserving of more attention. There are nuances in sport that are different to other industries that need to be progressed in the academic literature. It is timely to focus on ethics in sport entrepreneurship due to the increased interest in gender and sexuality discrimination. There is more emphasis on equality and support of diverse groups of society. Ethics can make a positive difference in sport as it enables a reflection about changes and perceptions of expected behavior. Sport is a popular form of activity to watch and participant in but cannot solve all societal problems. Instead sport can encourage more ethical conduct by educating people about best behavior. The field of sport entrepreneurship can incorporate an ethics perspective in order to contribute to a more interdisciplinary understanding of the nexus of sport with entrepreneurship. From an ethical perspective, sport is a way to address inequality and to foster better outcomes.

Researchers are encouraged to develop better measurement tools to evaluate the entrepreneurship in sport ethics. Finally, it must be noted that this chapter reports on the role entrepreneurship plays in sport ethics. Therefore, the findings are focused on the impact of innovation and change in sport ethics. This chapter will provide valuable insights for future sport managers wanting to utilize more entrepreneurial ethics. Future research needs to shed light on the ethics issues in sport and the interrelationship with entrepreneurship.

There is still much work to do about understanding the role of ethics in sport and how to nurture entrepreneurship. It is important to advance the current literature on sport ethics by investigating entrepreneurial behavior. Future generations will benefit from a more ethical form of sport participation. Thus, more research effort is needed on how to make sport organizations respond more entrepreneurially to ethical challenges. This might be done through targeting the cycle of ethics by learning about future trends. In addition, the intensity of ethics in sport remains subject to fluctuations. A meaningful research agenda is to focus on sport ethics from an entrepreneurial perspective. The lack of research about entrepreneurial effects of sport ethics does not represent what is occurring in the marketplace.

8.5   Conclusion

The relationship between sport ethics and entrepreneurship is the focus of this chapter. This chapter provides insights on the impacts of entrepreneurship on sport ethics policy through an investigation of how the research fields are linked. This chapter will contribute to the limited body of knowledge about the role of entrepreneurship in sport ethics by presenting a novel approach to understanding sport ethics by including an entrepreneurial perspective. This chapter contends that ethics and sport entrepreneurship have an interactive relationship and continues the discussion of sport entrepreneurship evident in the other chapters by going beyond current thinking of ethics to incorporate a more innovative perspective. The chapter highlights how in order to stimulate sport entrepreneurship there needs to be more interest in ethics. There is no definite answer as to how entrepreneurial forms of ethics are utilized in sport. Therefore, this chapter attempts to provide a starting point about how entrepreneurship is useful in a sport setting.

The outcome of this chapter are central to the acknowledgement of ethics being fundamental to the overall reputation of sport organizations. The future role of entrepreneurship in sport ethics will benefit from a more holistic approach. This is due to ethics defining the way sport is perceived in society. The findings of this chapter are noteworthy due to the development of a comprehensive understanding about the role entrepreneurship plays in sport ethics. This chapter has addressed the sport ethics-entrepreneurship nexus, and suggests that there will be more interest in this topic in the future. The stated aim of this chapter was to focus on entrepreneurship in sport ethics. The role of ethics has been researched widely in the business management literature but less in the sport entrepreneurship context. This has resulted in uncertainty about how sport ethics can be innovative, risk taking and proactive in the marketplace. There is room for sport entrepreneurs to utilize ethics as a way to solve business and societal problems. This chapter has discussed the role of ethics in sport entrepreneurship by taking a novel perspective about future developments. This chapter contributes to the entrepreneurship and sports management fields by adding an ethical perspective that is needed given the importance of the global sport industry to the economy. The issue of ethics needs to be continually investigated in terms of its application to sport. It is important to understand the ethical issues in sport and how they can be changed based on entrepreneurship.

References

Austin, M. W. (2017). Sport for the sake of the soul. *Sport, Ethics and Philosophy*. https://doi.org/10.1080/17511321.2017.1300604

Chell, E., Spence, L. J., Perrini, F., & Harris, J. D. (2016). Social entrepreneurship and business ethics: Does social equal ethical? *Journal of Business Ethics, 133*, 619–625.

Dey, P., & Steyaert, C. (2016). Rethinking the space of ethics in social entrepreneurship: Power, subjectivity, and practices of freedom. *Journal of Business Ethics, 133*(4), 627–641.

Edgar, A. (2013). Sport and art: An essay on the hermeneutics of sport. *Sport, Ethics and Philosophy, 7*(1), 1–9.

Hervieux, C., & Voltan, A. (2016). Framing social problems in social entrepreneurship. *Journal of Business Ethics*, 1–15. https://doi.org/10.1007/s10551-016-3252-1

Konig, E. (1995). Criticism of doping: The nihilistic side of technological sport and the antiquated view of sport ethics. *International Review for Sociology of Sport, 30*(3/4), 247–260.

Parnell, D., Spracklen, K., & Millward, P. (2017). Sport management issues in an era of austerity. *European Sport Management Quarterly, 17*(1), 67–74.

Russell, R., & Faulkner, B. (2004). Entrepreneurship, chaos, and the tourism area lifestyle. *Annals of Tourism Research, 31*(3), 556–579.

Schulenkorf, N. (2017). Managing sport-for-development: Reflections and outlook. *Sport Management Review, 20*, 243–251.

Shilbury, D., Sotiriadou, K., & Green, B. C. (2008). Sport development systems, policies and pathways: An introduction to the special issue. *Sport Management Review, 11*, 217–223.

Shogun, D., & Ford, M. (2000). A new sport ethics: Taking Konig seriously. *International Review for the Sociology of Sport, 35*(1), 49–58.

Sport Entrepreneurship Education and Policy

9.1 Introduction

There has been a growth in the number of students studying sport management at universities and an increase in the number of courses tied to sport. This is due to the increasing trend towards having a management qualification in sport and it being a prerequisite in terms of career progression. Sport managers operate at the professional, amateur and community level ensuring effective organization support but often need to behave in an entrepreneurial manner. In addition, there has been a growth in fitness and health activities in society caused by more interest in leisure time. This has led to more job opportunities around sport particularly for those self-employed and wanting to start sport related business ventures. The growth in 24 h gyms has further fuelled interest in the establishment of sport related businesses. Despite this increase, there has been little if any subjects on entrepreneurship in sport management courses. This has fueled the realization that entrepreneurship education is useful to sport students because of the integration of management training and teaching. In addition, athletes studying at educational institutions want to learn more about entrepreneurship because they will have to manage their own careers and this requires business acumen. This is due to entrepreneurship education incorporating skills such as creativity and innovation, which are useful in sports careers. Thus, there is a laggard effect in terms of what is happening in the sports marketplace and what is being taught in schools.

This chapter contributes to a better understanding of the linkage between entrepreneurship and sports education by proposing that there needs to be greater integration of these concepts. I hope that this chapter will inspire more interest in sports entrepreneurship education by suggesting that sport educators need to embrace an entrepreneurial supportive culture, which focuses on innovation and creativity. Embedding entrepreneurship into sports education enables a learning system to evolve over time that captures ingenuity and creativity. It is more effective to combine entrepreneurship and sports education in order to secure a better learning foundation for students. This chapter will first discuss the importance of entrepreneurship education in sport by highlighting the need for information in the knowledge

© Springer International Publishing AG 2018
V. Ratten, *Sport Entrepreneurship*, Management for Professionals,
https://doi.org/10.1007/978-3-319-73010-3_9

economy. Next, the role of entrepreneurial ecosystems to facilitate innovation and learning will be discussed followed by policy initiatives around sport education. The chapter concludes by suggesting how the future of sport management education needs to foster more entrepreneurial thinking.

9.2   Education

Education involves the setting in motion of the ability of people to access information or know how in order to gain information. As more information is available online people now need help as to where to get the information instead of knowing the information. This has resulted in an information revolution in which more knowledge is available in an open way but requires the right kind of analysis. Hence, knowledge is replacing capital as being the most important function in a sport organization and requires different kind of teaching in order to understand its application. This has led to more intellectual interest in emerging forms of knowledge and the impact they will have on the sports industry. Education plays an important part in this process for sport organizations and it is important that continual learning takes place. This is due to the knowledge society emphasizing the role of entrepreneurship in the education process.

Education provides the structure for enabling information about sport entrepreneurship to be shared in society. Education programs can be evaluated based on their coherence, efficacy, efficiency and relevance (Fayolle and Gailly 2015). Coherence involves examining whether the contents of the program suit the needs of individuals. This is important in ensuring the objectives are understood by the participants of a course. The pedagogical resources need to be appropriate and in the sport context relevant for the industry. Pedagogy includes the way a course is taught in terms of face-to-face learning and online learning. This is important in sport education as students need to have the learning capacity to engage in different types of knowledge. Efficacy means making sure the content taught meets the objectives of the course. People have different reasons for learning so it is important that these are understood by teachers. Efficiency means ensuring that the time spent in a course is on the right material. This is important in ensuring the learning resources are optimized. As time is a strategic weapon it is important it is used wisely in sports education. This means using the most appropriate resources given the time and cost restrictions. Relevance refers to whether the content of the course is relevant to the current industry conditions. In sport education, there are changing demands of businesses and consumers that need to be met through education. People will have different expectations about what they require from a sports course that should be acknowledged at the early stages. This means explaining and understanding the reasons for the inclusion of entrepreneurship in a course. In addition, the relevance of a sport course might be part of the upskilling or retraining that needs to occur due to the emerging technology changing the business landscape.

Entrepreneurship education can take a variety of forms from social, technological and international that can provide operational excellence to the sport industry. There are societal benefits from entrepreneurship education that can extend performance and enable knowledge transfer. For society it is important that issues around having a healthy lifestyle are embedded within entrepreneurship education. The technological forms of entrepreneurship education include using new media communication such as social channels to foster community engagements. Sport technology is changing rapidly and it is important that students are taught about future trends. International elements refer to the differences in culture, which affect entrepreneurship education. Some cultures value risk taking more than others, which needs to be taken into account by educational provides. Overall, the ultimate results of entrepreneurship education are employment generated by new entrepreneurial activity. Thus,, entrepreneurship education has a decisive role in developing better students prepared for the challenges in sport organizations. Organizing more entrepreneurship education programs about sport can contribute to the creation of new knowledge. This will enhance the outcomes of sport entrepreneurship education because they will be significant for the growth of new inventions.

The goal of entrepreneurship education is to help students acquire skills that are needed in today's changing business world. These skills will change based on available resources and time so the process of entrepreneurship is more important. Entrepreneurship is defined broadly as a mindset in education that focuses on behavior. In the sport context, entrepreneurship education can involve using experiential methods that develop problem solving skills. Thus, entrepreneurship education is important in sport as it fosters a can do attitude rather than rote learning. This is an important skill for students to develop as they need to be aware of how their behaviors influence outcomes.

Sport education has evolved over time due to the response of business and society needs. Whilst initially sport education was about physical activity the role of sport in society has broadened to focus on business activity and how it can prosper in an entrepreneurial society. In addition, different types of sport such as electronic sports have changed the way people perceive sport. This means that there needs to be a change in sport education teaching methods to reflect the entrepreneurial nature of the sport industry. In addition, there has been criticism of sports education in focusing too much on the physical aspects of sport rather than the philosophy behind sports. This is due to the emphasis on sport on strength and fitness rather than the softer side of sport such as engagement and fun. Moreover, sport has changed from being an amateur led activity to having more of a commercial focus. To facilitate better use of sports facilities many communities have created a set of institutions and government entities mandated with facilitating knowledge flow. Amateur sporting bodies still have a large amount of money to invest in best practices so entrepreneurial thinking can benefit them.

Education providers are institutions that influence business creation processes. North (1990: 3) defines institutions as "the rules of the game in a society, or more formally, institutions are the constraints that shape human interaction". In a sport context, institutions are at the heart of the industry as there is a lot of regulation and bureaucracy. Sport institutions are becoming more global due to the internet and global communication becoming easier. Another definition by Guerrero et al. (2011: 146) states "institutions can be either formal—such as political rules, economic rules, and contracts- or informal—such as codes of conduct, attitudes, values, norms of behavior, and conventions, or rather the culture of a specific society". Formal sport institutions are those established usually by the government to focus on a specific need such as health or a sport. The informal institutions are also important in sport due to the need for regulation about how to behave. Both formal and informal sport institutions engage in educational initiatives as they shape human interaction and the sharing of knowledge. For sport education, institutions provide a mechanism for ensuring learning standards and enabling entrepreneurial attitudes to develop.

Entrepreneurial attitudes are important in sport as they provide a way of undertaking initiatives. Sometimes it is hard for individuals to evaluate opportunities so entrepreneurship education is helpful. Education is crucial to sport as it facilitates a learning model that encourages inquisitiveness. This is important in harnessing the potential of sport as a way to change society for the better. Educational institutions reduce uncertainty by teaching people how to predict and respond to change in sport. This enables education to utilize human interaction to challenge thoughts and provide action plans. Education assists in increasing the learning capabilities and entrepreneurial intentions of individuals. This is important as innovations in sport need to be transmitted to a wider community audience. The sport industry needs to encourage more of an entrepreneurial spirit. Therefore, the importance of education for the sport industry is generally recognized but it needs to take a more entrepreneurial perspective. This is due to the big impact technology innovations have had on the sport industry. As a consequence more sport organizations are need education about how to be more entrepreneurial.

This chapter challenges the belief that sport and entrepreneurship education are separate subjects by suggesting that an entrepreneurial approach is needed in sport education. Due to the increasing role of sport as a career option there is a need for educators to teach entrepreneurship skills. More people are seeing sport as a career as there are financial and personal gains. In the past, many athletes had to work second jobs to support their sport career but this has changed. Now there is at the local and community level financial support for athletes to focus on sport and this has changed people's perceptions about sport careers as a reliable job. At the state and federal level there is also increasing amounts of funding to support athletes in their supporting careers. This has been a source of controversy in some countries like Australia as students need to pay for higher education but in many cases sport education is subsidized. In addition, in sports considered lifestyle or adventure focuses there has been a change with athletes in these sports now earning large amounts of money. Therefore, the role of sport as a viable career option has altered and the resulting need for entrepreneurship education has increased.

9.3   Sports Entrepreneurship Education

Education is a legitimate way to learn about new trends and solutions to sport issues. Yet in the sport education literature there is little acknowledgement of entrepreneurship. Entrepreneurship education suggests that there needs to be new and continual change to come up with the best solutions. This means that sport education should be concerned with creating an entrepreneurial ecosystem to support new knowledge. Entrepreneurship education in sport provides a powerful way to incorporate business training and foster more interest in economic issues. This is evident in entrepreneurship creating an ecosystem through having a support structure and an infrastructure framework.

The role of sports entrepreneurship education is to share knowledge about how to create new businesses and commercialize in the sports environment. This involves increasing information about the role of entrepreneurship in sport from the private to non-profit forms of organizations.Education serves as a conduit to facilitate the spillover of knowledge that can generate innovative activity. This is due to knowledge being the driving factor underlying sport growth and performance. Knowledge is important as a way to achieve a competitive advantage in the sport industry. Moreover, education plays a significant role in sport but just focusing on physical aspects of sport does not suffice in generating knowledge about business creation. The emergence of sport entrepreneurship education is needed to provide solutions to global and social problems.

Sports entrepreneurship education is a new interdisciplinary field that can facilitate the spillover of knowledge from sport to other sectors. The knowledge spillovers come from a number of factors impacting sport education from physical conditions to psychological determinants. The role of entrepreneurship in sports education is fundamental to the generation of sport startups and new ventures. This enables sports entrepreneurship education to provide leadership and innovative thinking. Sports education can be enhanced by entrepreneurial capital that enables people to thrive in the knowledge economy.

It is worth exploring the role of entrepreneurship education in sport due to its ability to fill a gap in the pedagogical methods that is currently missing in many courses. This is due to innovation being embedded in sport organizations and fostering the interaction between different sectors of an economy. The triple helix is a way of understanding the role of entrepreneurship education. This reflects the collaboration between government, industry and university in the functioning of the knowledge economy. Society is also sometimes referred to as the fourth helix due to its impact on university arrangements. In sport education there has been a tendency to leave out entrepreneurship in the discussion due to entrenched teaching methods. This is surprising as education needs to take a more entrepreneurial perspective and utilize the triple helix to foster sport engagement.

The products and services by sport organizations have changed over the years due to the emergence of the fitness and lifestyle sector. This has created challenges for sport educators in terms of the subjects they teach. Sport educators need to be proactive contributors to the advancement of the industry especially in the global knowledge driven economy. This means sport educators need to expand their teaching methods beyond traditional topics to incorporate more innovative methods. This involves the interaction between universities, government, industry and society in order to change sport education.

Employers are requiring graduates to have a more proactive attitude to change and this is where entrepreneurship education becomes useful. Educators need to provide entrepreneurship training in order that graduates are ready for the workforce. In the past there was a focus on theoretical aspects of sport education but this should change to incorporate a more entrepreneurial approach. There are different types of education providers from practical training colleges to universities that are all competing for student enrollments. The new sport educators have somewhat filled the gaps in the marketplace by offering services related to business training. Traditional educators like universities have been slower to integrate entrepreneurship education into sport management curriculum due to the focus on other subject areas.

New technologies in sport and the education sector have had an impact on sport educators. This is due to technology innovation becoming integral to the functioning of the sport industry. There are mobile communication applications and websites that play a key role in the sport sector. Students need to learning about these new and emerging technologies in their courses in order to be able to use them in future employment positions. In addition, sport educators need to rethink their roles in enabling a more entrepreneurial learning environment.

Sport organizations are embedded in a global network of stakeholders who need to collaborate but also compete. In order to play an important role in society sport organizations need to have people who can understand the complexity of their businesses. Sport businesses have a multi-functional business model with online communications complemented by traditional product and service offerings. Therefore, more sport organizations need to change their view of intellectual capital by fostering more education programs. This involves strategic partnerships with educational providers to help them share knowledge and engage in a learning community. This will help to enable learning as a constant activity in sport so education plays an important role. History is part of the sport industry and organizations can learn from it. Whilst sport in its history has had an entrepreneurial nature it needs to be more overt in the learning tools. This is due to entrepreneurial behaviours needing to be an integral part of the mission of sport organizations. To achieve this entrepreneurship education needs to be recognized as a form of competitive advantage.

Entrepreneurship requires cooperation between different entities involved in sport. Learning is central to the development of sport organizations who can utilize connections to facilitate the sharing of knowledge. Sport organizations have different aims and objectives that impact on their willingness to utilize entrepreneurship education. The role of teaching is an important part of sport management but has often been neglected in terms of its importance for the competitiveness of the sport industry. As sport has evolved to include lifestyle applications, the demands of educators have increased. Sport is a hothouse for technology innovation and

startups that impact economic development. Thus, the complexity of sports entrepreneurship means that more education is required to adhere to the traditional
knowledge sources but also integrate new information. This will enable sport to
adapt to the needs of society by enabling it to be entrepreneurial.

More sport students are realizing that they can have an entrepreneurial career. The
awareness of entrepreneurship is based on the increased importance of sport business.
Education plays an important role in influencing the entrepreneurial intentions of
sport students. There are entrepreneurial behaviours in the characteristics of sport
students due to their interest in fitness and health activities. Thus, sport education and
entrepreneurship have a mutual relationship through the exchanging of knowledge.
Environmental changes in sport have lead to an increased interest in technology
transfer and commercialization. There are more sport applications on mobile phones
and mobile commerce, which has meant a growth in different types of business.

Education is seen as having a key role in the sport sector and can encourage
entrepreneurship. In the sport sector there is a wider need to generate individuals
who can work in both the commercial and public sector. This is due to most people
staying in jobs for shorter time periods than the past and there is an expectation that
people will change jobs. In addition, there is uncertainty about people's careers now
due to the changing business environment. This means that entrepreneurship
education is utilized as a way for individuals to learn about changing career options.
This includes entrepreneurial business planning that can be taught in the sport
sector. Business planning is a key part of entrepreneurship education, which brings
sport students into more contact with business. This enables students to develop the
skills needed to start or manage a business. In addition, entrepreneurship education
incorporates experiential learning through case studies and practical applications.
Internships are often popular for sport students and with these job placements come
a need to know the practical and business side of the business.

There is a need to reform sport education by making it more entrepreneurial.
This can be conducted by having an entrepreneurial vision about sports education.
A purpose-orientated approach to sports education demands an entrepreneurial
pedagogy that challenges current thinking. By connecting the entrepreneurship
and sport management education fields there can be a revolution. This enables the
expression of sports education as entrepreneurial. More experimentation with
entrepreneurial teaching methods would be useful to sport students. This is due to
entrepreneurship education providing a more business and real world approach to
sport studies. Entrepreneurship education can create value to sport organizations by
providing new thought leadership, which is needed in the industry.

At the heart of entrepreneurship education is learning about how to create and
transfer knowledge. Entrepreneurship needs to be introduced into more sport
education courses as it can facilitate the learning about new ideas and concerns
about future trends. This enables sport education to contribute to societal advancement by teaching students how to anticipate and foresee change in the marketplace.
Sport educators need to have policies in place to facilitate a move towards more
entrepreneurship study. This will facilitate new relationships between stakeholders

in a sports context. Thus, entrepreneurship education efforts need to focus on how sport can leverage more innovation outcomes.

Entrepreneurship education should be a strategic priority for sport managers. This will help remove existing prejudices and transform individuals into entrepreneurs. Becoming good at entrepreneurship will enable sport managers to perform better in the marketplace. This can help create competitive advantages and motivate sport leaders to behave in a more proactive manner. There is ample support for the assertion that more entrepreneurship training is needed in sport. This is due to entrepreneurship facilitating a competitive advantage that can enrich the sport industry.

Sport educators need to try to adapt to changing environmental conditions by incorporating entrepreneurship studies into the curriculum. Educators cannot depend on traditional models to teach sport and need to change to a more entrepreneurial learning approach. This is due to people working in the sport industry needing to be quicker in responding to environmental change. Typically most sport education programs focused on the physical aspects without relating to the outside business world. By incorporating entrepreneurship training in sport, educators can diversify their learning models to be more adaptive. This helps build an entrepreneurial culture in sport that enables people to react positively to change. Sport educators that embrace change can help build a more entrepreneurial identify in their courses. Moreover, sport students need to be taught how to react under market pressure. By teaching entrepreneurship sport students can survive in the global market by keeping a relevant place in society. Much of the sport entrepreneurship education can be conducted at universities as they have a closer link to the working life of students.

9.4   Entrepreneurial Sport Universities

Entrepreneurship education has tended to focus on new business development and internationalization without including the societal roles that are being more recognized at universities whose mission is to bring theoretical concepts and real world training together. This has changed with increased interest in social and sustainable forms of entrepreneurship, which are vital to the development of the global economy. At universities entrepreneurship education has tended to focus on licensing agreements, spin-off ventures and technology transfer typically popular in the sciences. This focus has changed with universities realizing that sport related activities such as patents, medical advancements and community engagement are also important. Moreover, sport teams at a university impact on brand image and reputation. This affects student enrolments and the ranking of a university. In addition, alumni engagement and endowments are often tied to the performance of sport teams at a university. Most of the well known university sport teams tend to come from the big United States universities such as Ohio State or Florida State. However, smaller university sport teams also play an important role in the social and economic development of a community. An example is Marshall University in West Virginia who is famous for their football team. In the past the role of university sport was generally confined to on field game performance. However, related activities such as television broadcasts and merchandise sales now account for a large source of university income. Computer games featuring university sport stars are popular in addition to memorabilia.

Recently there has been an increased interest in entrepreneurial universities that teach, mentor and help both students and the wider community. Etzkowitz (2013: 487) states "theories of the university typically fail to account for the metamorphosis of a medieval institution based on charitable and eleemosynary principles into one capable of generating regional economic growth". Therefore, the change in focus for universities to more interest on entrepreneurship has been the result of the digital and knowledge economy. This has meant the transmission of information is a strategic weapon that needs to be disseminated in a smart way. Therefore, the changing of teaching methods typically lecture focused to more blended learning methods that incorporate online communication. This has impacted sport studies but there is still reluctance by many universities to change their teaching methods to incorporate more entrepreneurship.

Sport has been a beneficiary of the entrepreneurial economy as more technology has crept into the industry. As Guerrero et al. (2015: 748) states "the entrepreneurial economy is not confined to the role of small businesses and business owners, but also it is the pervasive, socio-economic mindset of thinking". This is evident in the entrepreneurial economy fostering sports related technology products and services becoming more popular in the marketplace. Universities provide the ecosystem as they connect different stakeholders together in a collaborativbe manner.

Entrepreneurial universities adapt to environmental change by encouraging innovative and creative activities. This means risk is considered as necessary for growth but needs to be managed in the appropriate manner. Sport ventures can be risky but need experimentation in order to evolve. Universities provide a good environment for sport entrepreneurship due to the existence of infrastructure and services. This enables sport entrepreneurs to explore opportunities but utilize university resources such as knowledge and expertise to progress their ideas. Guerrero et al. (2015: 751) define human capital as "the stock of competences, knowledge, abilities and skills gained through education and training". Entrepreneurial universities realize that sport ventures need the appropriate amount and type of human capital. Therefore, students, alumni, athletes and educators can work together at a university in order to foster an entrepreneurial ecosystem.

In the sport industry, there are both formal and informal relationships with universities. This is due to the need for collaborative research in sport. Universities play a role in facilitating the generation and dissemination of sport knowledge. It is important that universities and sport organizations actively participate in the process of collaboration. This is due to there being some problems sometimes amongst stakeholders of sport organizations in collaboration and sharing knowledge. However, in order to progress there needs to be the initiation and maintenance of collaboration amongst sport entities and entrepreneurial universities. For this to take place there needs to be the appropriate sport policy that fosters entrepreneurship education.

9.5   Sport Policy

There is a focus in sport policy on diversity issues but more emphasis is increasingly focusing on entrepreneurship. This is due to some sports being focused on certain stereotypes without considering the marginalized sector of society. Fink and Pastore (1999: 310) in discussing diversity in sport state "the maintenance of the status quo goes beyond demographics and that homologous reproduction exists in attitudes, values and leadership". Thus, it is important to take a fresh perspective to sport policy by focusing on entrepreneurship as a way of fostering anti-discrimination. Discrimination in sport concerns age, disability, gender, race and sexual orientation (Fink and Pastore 1999). These different forms of discrimination can be lowered if sport educators focus on ways to bring about more societal inclusion.

Sport due to its pervasive nature in society requires policy analysis and management in terms of discrimination and inclusion. There are different types of policies applied to sport from environmental, global to innovative. These policies develop based on changes in the market and societal expectations around sport funding and sport. Policy analysts utilize sport to help heal rifts in the community caused by different forms of discrimination. Sport is considered a global language that transcends political, cultural and social differences. Thus, entrepreneurial ways to utilize sport policy can help foster better educational programs.

Sport policy has developed from cultural, historical and social legacies. Different countries and types of sports have had better success with policy initiatives. This is due to the perceived need of sport to contribute to community well-being and development. In countries such as Australia, there is a strong emphasis on sport due to the cultural connotations of sport in society. This has meant more funding has gone towards sport due to its role in the political system. This is evident in countries like Australia has had a good sport policy in conjunction with the Australian Institute of Sport. Some countries have more funding towards sport policy due to the cultural position of sport in their society. Thus, educational initiatives in these more sport proactive countries can utilize entrepreneurial initiatives.

Sport policy is based on the need for institutionalization and regulation within society. De Bosscher et al. (2009) proposed the sport policy factors that lead to international sporting success model as a way to analyse sport policy form a global perspective. The government plays an important role in sport by suggesting changes and shaping its development. Thus, governments are constantly analyzing sport in terms of its identity and conceptualization in society. This has resulted in sport policy often aiming to find the causes or problems in sport by suggesting change. Future plans about sport are derived from ideas generated from political issues in sport.

There are implications for sport policy makers associated with having an entrepreneurial policy. This comes from the need to facilitate more knowledge and technology transfer between sport entities. Government involvement in sport has dual purposes in emphasizing both individual and society benefits from participation in sport. The individual benefits from sport come from the development of traits such as team work, discipline and hard work. These skills are important to the healthy functioning of society. Moreover, sport is considered as a neutral environment where people compete on skills. This is important in fostering social interaction based on goodwill and integrity. Coalter (2010: 296) views sport as "an apolitical, neutral and inherently integrative set of social practices that can deliver a wide range of positive outcomes". This means sport can be used to foster a range of policies from social inclusion and healthier lifestyles. Sport is seen as more than just an activity but rather a symbol or way of life.

Public policies about sport have increased with the growing awareness of the way sport transcends cultural and social barriers. Green and Collins (2008: 225) states "sport and government have been inextricably linked across a diverse range of policy issues including health, social inclusion, community development, education and the achievement of elite sporting success". Sport policy is changing to be more entrepreneurial due to the interest in creating opportunities that are innovative and forward thinking. Typically most sport policy is based on politics and this can be utilized in educational programs to foster community engagement.

Nygard and Gates (2013) suggest that the mechanisms for sport diplomacy include image building, building a platform for dialogue, trust building, reconciliation, integration and anti-racism. Thus, sport policy can be utilized in cross-cultural discussions as sport is a source of leisure and recreation for people. Entrepreneurship can help strengthen the bridge between sport and policy interventions. Thus, the effectiveness of sport policy depends on the way entrepreneurship is embedded into programs. This includes using sport policy as a way of changing current management and societal practices.

Governments manage sport policy through advisory committees, commissions of inquiry and taskforces. This enables sport policy to be linked to a wide range of social issues that impact a community. Moreover, there are different aims of sport policy from efficiency, equality, fairness and universality. These aims have different meanings according to the stakeholders involved as sport has long played a crucial role in a nation's identity. Policy is important in influencing specific areas of sport that need to be changed. Government policies around sport tend to be formal and written in documents based on research. However, there is also informal polices that are important in sport but less well known.

Sport policy is used for a number of objectives through interventionist means. Sport is considered an instrumental policy tool because of its malleable nature (Green 2006). Green (2006: 218) states sport is "an aspect of socio-cultural development related to a wide range of welfare services including education, health, social services, land-use planning and the arts". There needs to be a policy shift in sport to focus more on entrepreneurship. There are expectations from bureaucrats and practitioners about the role entrepreneurship can play in sport policy. This is due to entrepreneurship offering new perspectives about the role policy plays in sport development.

Green (2006) suggests that sport policy has shifted from a focus on providing sport to everyone to more of a focus on elite and performance aspects. This is based on governments interested in their global competitive position and the fostering of best practice standards. Sport policy priorities have shifted to be more performance orientated with tangible outcomes. This is due to governments facing more scrutiny about financing and the public wanting to see results. Entrepreneurship can be a prominent and guiding way to influence sport policy. The reason behind emphasizing entrepreneurship in sport policy is due to its ability to transform different parts of society. Thus, a compelling rationale for entrepreneurship in policy is the focus on future trends that will impact the sport sector. Entrepreneurship is a coherent policy that can be used as an umbrella term for a range of sport objectives. This includes social issues that have diverse applications in sport. This is becoming more relevant with the constant shift in sports technology that can also be characterized as entrepreneurial policy.

Entrepreneurial thinking needs to be welcomed into sport policy. Sam and Jackson (2006: 366) states "the value placed on citizen involvement in policy making ebbs and flows". Thus, entrepreneurship will become a prominent feature in sport policy debates in the future due to its ability to forecast citizen sentiment, government needs and societal concerns. Individuals participate in sport policy decisions through advisory councils, boards, committees, professional associations and trade unions (Sam and Jackson 2006).

Sport entrepreneurship involves discovering unfulfilled needs in the market that can support change. This involves assembling networks of organizations and individuals that can facilitate innovation. Part of this process involves risk as ideas are generated and then put into practice. Anderson and Ronglan (2015) posit that there are two levels of entrepreneurial strategies: organizational and system. Both of these strategies can be utilized in entrepreneurial sport policy around education. Thus, as innovation is a precursor to entrepreneurship it is important to incorporate this into sport policy.

The growth of the sport industry has necessitated more focus on the policies around the conduct of players on and off the field. This is due to more interest in the interaction between customers, coaches and players and the community in the sport context. Some of the education policies have tended to have an innovative perspective due to the need for a more futuristic thinking in the sport industry. Innovation in sport policy helps to generate new behaviours that are needed in response to environmental change and educational demand. This includes developing policies around the growth of new sport ideas in terms of playing conditions and educational courses.

Successful sport organizations look to implement policies that are reflective of current market conditions and help support future needs. There are internal policies a sport organization needs to consider in terms of its competitiveness. These include polices around nutrition as it affects performance. Professional sport clubs have nutritionists and psychologists to help increase performance. However, more recently there have been controversial issues around the use of performance enhancement products many of which are unregulated. This means sport clubs need to be proactive about predicting whether the use of a product will be inline with regulations or should be avoided.

9.6   Conclusion

In terms of the future, there are several avenues of importance to sport entrepreneurship education and policy makers. Sport policy scholars should undertake more studies utilizing entrepreneurship theory in order to improve their own research. This would help tap into the wider debate about the usefulness of sport policy in society. The studying of entrepreneurship in sport policy is important as a way to understand the business development process. Therefore, sport policy scholars have much work to do in terms of contribution to policy and entrepreneurship study debates. This will enable sport entrepreneurship theory to be integrated more into policy studies.

This chapter represents a practical and theoretical contribution to sport entrepreneurship and education studies. There needs to be a fundamental change in the current way sport is taught by encouraging an entrepreneurship perspective. Many people in the sport sector take an entrepreneurial approach to work and this should be taught to current sport students. This chapter is amongst the first to explicitly connect sports entrepreneurship with education thereby connecting separate fields. More work is needed to understand the relationship between sport policy and entrepreneurship education in order to provide better teaching methods.

This chapter sketches a new field of sport entrepreneurship education by discussing the lack of literature connecting sport entrepreneurship and education. Sport educators need to utilize entrepreneurship as a contextual framework for further policy discussion. More schools and universities need to utilize entrepreneurship education in sport studies because of its practical application. Educational institutions can include entrepreneurship in sport studies thereby transforming existing pedagogy.

References

Andersen, S. S., & Ronglan, L. T. (2015). Historical paths and policy change: Institutional entrepreneurship in Nordic elite sport systems. *International Journal of Sport Policy and Politics, 7*(2), 197–216.

Coalter, F. (2010). The politics of sport-for-development: Limited focus programmes and broad gauge problems? *International Review for the Sociology of Sport, 45*(3), 295–314.

De Bosscher, V., De Knop, P., Van Bottenburg, M., Shibli, S., & Bingham, J. (2009). Explaining international sporting success: An international comparison of elite sport systems and policies in six countries. *Sport Management Review, 12*(3), 113–136.

Etzkowitz, H. (2013). Anatomy of the entrepreneurial university. *Social Science Information, 52* (3), 486–511.

Fayolle, A., & Gailly, B. (2015). The impact of entrepreneurship education on entrepreneurial attitudes and intentions: Hysteresis and persistence. *Journal of Small Business Management, 53*(1), 75–93.

Fink, J. S., & Pastore, D. L. (1999). Diversity in sport? Utilizing the business literature to devise a comprehensive framework of diversity initiatives. *Quest, 51*(4), 310–327.

Green, M. (2006). From 'sport for all' to not about sport at all?: Interrogating sport policy interventions in the United Kingdom. *European Sport Management Quarterly, 6*(3), 217–238.

Green, M., & Collins, S. (2008). Policy, politics and path dependence: Sport development in Australia and Finland. *Sport Management Review, 11*, 225–251.

Guerrero, M., Toledano, N., & Urbano, D. (2011). Entrepreneurial universities and support mechanisms: A Spanish case study. *International Journal of Entrepreneurship and Innovation Management, 13*(2), 144–160.

Guerrero, M., Cunningham, J. A., & Urbano, D. (2015). Economic impact of entrepreneurial universities activities: An exploratory study of the United Kingdom. *Research Policy, 44*, 748–764.

North, D. C. (1990). *Institutions, institutional change and economic performance*. Cambridge: University Press.

Nygard, H. M., & Gates, S. (2013). Soft power at home and abroad: Sport diplomacy, politics and peace building. *International Area Studies Review, 16*(3), 235–243.

Sam, M. P., & Jackson, S. J. (2006). Developing national sport policy through consultation: The rules of engagement. *Journal of Sport Management, 20*, 366–386.

The Future for Sport Entrepreneurship

10

10.1 Introduction

The inspiration for this book comes from the lack of research work combining sport and entrepreneurship. This means that sport entrepreneurship research requires new directions that resonate with practice. This book is timely as it will explore new frontiers within sport entrepreneurship. Some of the key issues about sport entrepreneurship are discussed to reflect upon important areas on inquiry. The further consideration of sport entrepreneurship can contribute to future investigations about the role of emerging technologies and new business practices. More study of innovation related businesses in sport could produce better practical knowledge for various stakeholders. In the future, researchers can use different types of entrepreneurship to review the linkages with sport from different viewpoints.

Given the dearth of research on sports entrepreneurship, I was motivated to write this book. The growth of sport entrepreneurship is rising in most countries around the world. The reality is that sport entrepreneurship is young and still in the development phase. This book will capture the uniqueness of sport entrepreneurship in order to progressively build the field. The future for sports entrepreneurship research is optimistic given the interest in the field. This book enables the prioritization of the collaborative process between sport organizations and entrepreneurial behavior. Thus, the concept of sport entrepreneurship is an innovative way to tackle the increasing dependence of innovation for competitiveness in sport organizations. More work is needed to understand why sport organizations are entrepreneurial as not all are involved in innovation. The findings of this book constitute an important area for future research about sport entrepreneurship and how it generates knowledge spillovers to other sectors of the economy.

Sports entrepreneurship has a positive influence on organizations as it enables practical change. This is due to sport entrepreneurs positioning themselves in a way that goes beyond current management practices. Entrepreneurship is a major mechanism of change in sport. This book discusses sport entrepreneurship, which is a promising avenue for future research. There are commonalities between the entrepreneurship and sport management literature that can provide insights for sport

© Springer International Publishing AG 2018
V. Ratten, *Sport Entrepreneurship*, Management for Professionals,
https://doi.org/10.1007/978-3-319-73010-3_10

entrepreneurship research. In this book, I propose that the sport industry has created favorable conditions for entrepreneurship, initiating shifts in the types of products and services entering the marketplace. Thus, this book contributes to practice as it gathers the way sport and entrepreneurship can be used by managers in their organizations. There are also theoretical contributions coming from this book due to its continued discussion of a theory of sport-based entrepreneurship.

There has been increasing acknowledgement of the use of entrepreneurship in the successful transformation of the industry (Palalic et al. 2017). The intention to be entrepreneurial in sport can take a variety of forms that provide practical and real life benefits. This is due to the realization that sport entrepreneurship takes a variety of forms. An updated body of knowledge around sport entrepreneurship is needed to assist in the development of this field. This would recognize the advantages and disadvantages of entrepreneurship in sport. Thus, there is the possibility to explore how entrepreneurship is affecting sport in different contexts such as education and training. An example is that more entrepreneurs are starting their own businesses based on their passion and knowledge about sport. Over time, as entrepreneurship education programs focus on sport there will be more attention on sports entrepreneurs. This will mean that as the field moves forward, researchers face the choice of which aspect of entrepreneurship they want to study in a sports context.

The sports entrepreneurship literature is at its infancy and young in terms of development. This means there is a lack of understanding about the definition and types of sports entrepreneurship. There are two main approaches to sports entrepreneurship. The first approach focuses on intentions to solve sport problems that require innovative thinking. This means that persistent issues plaguing the sport industry can be addressed through entrepreneurship. More sport organizations are using entrepreneurship to ensure they have better outcomes to stressing issues. This is due to the efforts of sport managers balancing both economic and social aspects. The important topics about sport studied through entrepreneurship include small business management and new venture intentions. There is some debate about the notion of entrepreneurship in relationship to sport due to the way sport is embedded in society. Today, sport entrepreneurship researchers present the idea that entrepreneurship is critical for sport. This has enabled more sport scholars to use the term entrepreneurship as an umbrella theme to study a range of contexts.

Understanding the factors influencing sport entrepreneurship is the central theme of this book. Taken together the chapters focus on sport entrepreneurship and the mechanisms that shape performance outcomes. By studying the sport industry and types of entrepreneurship, the chapters provide a holistic understanding of the implications of entrepreneurship in sport. I hope that the chapters provide numerous opportunities for continued interest in sport entrepreneurship. This book will encourage intellectual engagement with the entrepreneurship and sport management disciplines. By combining entrepreneurship and sport the book provides a cohesive and comprehensive way to understand the connection.

In this book, I suggest that sport entrepreneurship involves innovative activity from knowledge that is generated in a sports context. Thus, this book provides considerable insights about sport entrepreneurship by discussing the ample opportunities for further research. Sport entrepreneurship is an emerging area of sport and entrepreneurship studies that will continue to gain traction in the future. Whilst sport entrepreneurship is needed in society, there is still uncertainty about is nature and role. In this book, I outline how sports entrepreneurship is emerging as a novel field filling the void between entrepreneurship and sport management research. A key issue about sports entrepreneurship is how will it develop in the future? This question is relevant as the academic discourse on sport entrepreneurship has been sparse due to the confusion about its role in business research. Sport entrepreneurship is alluring as it enables transformation to take place that combines innovation with business creation.

This book draws on both theory and practice to provide a balanced view of sport entrepreneurship. Careful attention needs to be placed on how sport entrepreneurship is different to other types of entrepreneurship. This book provides a comprehensive view of the important filed of sport entrepreneurship. The topic of sport entrepreneurship is complex and this book reviews its importance in society. I wrote this book as I felt there was a lack of consensus about what the term 'sport entrepreneurship' meant and also due to the burgeoning interest in the field. Sport entrepreneurship is difficult and hard work to most of the individuals and organizations involved. This book will make it possible for people to learn about sport entrepreneurship.

There is a depth of discussion about the various areas of sport entrepreneurship that provides a significant contribution to the field. The key premise of this book is viewing sport entrepreneurship as an area of practice rather than pure theory. The sport environment is constantly changing and those that survive are entrepreneurial. Sport entrepreneurs need to monitor change in terms of evaluating potential opportunities. Often the words entrepreneurship and innovation are used interchangeably due to the focus on change. In this book, I view entrepreneurship as relating to business ventures whilst innovation is doing something new. Hence, sport entrepreneurship inherently involves some innovation in order for it to progress. This book enables a new way to see entrepreneurship through a sport lens. I hope this book helps implement co-created solutions between the entrepreneurship and sport fields.

This book provides a range of inter-disciplinary perspectives about sport entrepreneurship in order to enrich the exchanging and disseminating of ideas. Entrepreneurship is a key enabler for the creation of business value. It is unclear what the drivers for sport entrepreneurship are and to know how organizations can develop creative thinking in a sports context. The aim of this book is to explore the concept of sport entrepreneurship and to generate new insights. This book does this by providing ways to see the combination of sport and entrepreneurship in new forms. The lessons in this book provide a way of understanding the emergence of sport entrepreneurship. This book provides a way to see sport entrepreneurship from a different perspective. The agenda of this book was to provide more interactions between the entrepreneurship and sport management disciplines. In doing so, the book examined how sports entrepreneurship is co-evolving from the linkage with the global economy.

10.2   Objectives of the Book

This book focuses on both empirical research and theory development about sport entrepreneurship. This enables fresh insights into the existing and new area of sports entrepreneurship. The chapters in this book will help to illuminate entrepreneurship in sport and lay a more holistic foundation for the discipline. This is due to entrepreneurship being the way that sport organizations will move forward. Yet it is interesting there is very little research on entrepreneurship in sport despite its impact on economic development. Thus, the potential usefulness of using entrepreneurship as a theoretical lens in sport has been largely ignored. This book fills this gap by making an effort to link sport to entrepreneurship. Moreover, this book helps to understand the contextual nature of sport so the role of entrepreneurship can be stressed. It is useful to examine sports institutions as they apply the rules and regulations that organizations need to follow. Thus, entrepreneurial policies of sport institutions are an insightful way to understand sports entrepreneurship.

I am confident that this book will help future researchers produce more robust understandings of sport entrepreneurs. In addition, I hope this book will play a crucial role in nurturing new research directions that provide a holistic view of sport entrepreneurship. A vital way to move the field of sport entrepreneurship ahead is to focus on defining its key attributes, whilst making it distinctive compared to other types of entrepreneurship. This is due to sports entrepreneurship providing value to other business management disciplines. Given the powerful role sport plays in the global economy it is important to highlight is entrepreneurial characteristics. Hopefully the future of sports entrepreneurship will use this book as a way to enrich more research work on this growing area.

This book collectively does an admirable job of focusing on new perspectives of sport entrepreneurship. By offering new explanations for entrepreneurship in sport the book provides a way to signify the importance of future research on this area. A debatable question is where the sport environment produces different types of entrepreneurship? This is due to the differences in the way entrepreneurship is considered in sport due to the role of innovation. Sports with a greater emphasis on technology for competitiveness will utilize more entrepreneurship. Thus, sport entrepreneurship makes a technical contribution by providing a contextual background. This helps to structure the research on sport entrepreneurship by providing a viewpoint on how sport needs innovation to improve competitiveness. This is important as sport organizations are empowered through their entrepreneurial activity.

This book is realistic about the role of entrepreneurship in sport but also futuristic in suggesting ways to move the research forward and in new directions. Sport entrepreneurship research needs to move more towards being published and accepted in well-known journal outlets and business practitioner publications. The contribution of this book is shown in the complexity of sports entrepreneurship, in terms of how it is culturally embedded. Therefore, this book enables a better understanding of the value of sports entrepreneurship to the global community. This is due to there being a rapidly emerging research stream connecting sport to entrepreneurship.

This book sets out to highlight the value of sports entrepreneurship for business management scholars and practitioners. This book will discuss a range of issues, questions and themes around sport entrepreneurship. Thereby making a contribution to the study of sports entrepreneurship and enabling a development in the body of knowledge. Sport entrepreneurship offers many opportunities for future research by extending our current thinking. This book is timely from a policy perspective as sport is a key component of the economy. There has been a shift towards more policy orientation towards public/private partnerships and sport has been a recipient of this attention (Ramadani et al. 2015). Thus, sport policy is useful in addressing social challenges and ways to integrate technological innovation.

The contents of this book contribute to the sport entrepreneurship literature in a number of ways. The greatest contribution of this book is providing a holistic understanding of how entrepreneurial behavior influences the sport industry. The consideration of entrepreneurship in sport will enable more theory building and practical understanding in the field of sport entrepreneurship. This book will contribute to the literature about sport entrepreneurship by examining the role of innovation in the creativity process. New insights from this book can better inform the sport industry about emerging practices. This will help build innovative perspectives around sport entrepreneurship.

10.3   The Future of Sports Entrepreneurship

Sport managers often ignore the value of innovative ideas and their effect on future performance. The close relationship sport managers often have with their environment may help to disseminate innovations into the marketplace. Thus, when sport managers disseminate information the resulting innovations can flow into the marketplace at a faster rate. There has been a recent emphasis on entrepreneurship in sport due to the commercialization and internationalization activities. This book builds on the innovation and sport literatures to address how businesses, governments and individuals can deliver sport entrepreneurship.

There are a number of general observations about the future of sports entrepreneurship. Firstly, there are many different types of sport entrepreneurship including corporate that should be studied as separate research areas in conjunction with more general types of entrepreneurship. The noteworthy areas of sport entrepreneurship tend to be more specific forms such as how companies evolve. This enables exploration about how sport entrepreneurship is distinctive when combined with more well researched areas of entrepreneurship. In addition, there is a need for more detailed analysis about how the networks existing in sport facilitate entrepreneurship. This will take into consideration the network structures of the sport industry that create innovation.

Secondly, the knowledge creation process in sport needs to be observed from different perspectives such as athletes, managers and employees. These people have different perceptions about the effects of innovation and use of creativity for sport management (Ratten et al. 2017). Increased usages of technology in sport have made communication and sharing of knowledge easier. It would be interesting to see the effects of knowledge dissemination within and between sport organizations. Entrepreneurship research has grown in significance over the past decade with its growing impact on other disciplines (Ratten and Dana 2017). Most of the existing entrepreneurship research is limited to general management studies but this has been changing. There is a lack of linkage to sport in entrepreneurship research, which requires further attention. In particularly, little is known about the entrepreneurial process in sport and how it is used in a sports context to advance performance.

Thirdly, there are many environmental factors impacting sports entrepreneurship that depend on market conditions. This includes internal organizational factors such as relationships and work environment, which impact sport innovation. External organizational factors include economic and regulatory conditions that influence the degree of innovation. Hence, more understanding of the various environmental effects on sport entrepreneurship is required. Sport entrepreneurship is at its early stage of theoretical development and except for the past few years has been invisible in much mainstream business management research. The paucity of research on sport entrepreneurship contradicts the contemporary media view of sport as being entrepreneurial.

There will be a rapid expansion on research about sport entrepreneurship as it is a typical and interesting area to study. This will help to create an active research community amongst scholars of sport entrepreneurship. In addition, the vibrancy of sport entrepreneurship research means there are many different ways to capture new directions that provide a richer understanding of the field. This book will encourage new directions for research on sport entrepreneurship that (a) studies new environmental contexts for sport entrepreneurship in terms of countries, industries and sports, (b) produces new theoretical frameworks for understanding the process of sport entrepreneurship at an individual, organization and regional level, (c) uses new epistemology and methodological approaches to analyse the development of sport entrepreneurship and (d) improves on the linkage between sport and entrepreneurship by focusing on the creativity process.

Most of the existing research published on sport entrepreneurship has tended to be conceptual and theoretical in nature. This has changed more recently with the use of sport-based entrepreneurship theory in empirical studies. Whilst these recent studies have advanced the field of sport entrepreneurship, there is a need to continue maintaining the research projection of this topic. Exploring entrepreneurship in the context of sport organizations enables a way to see entrepreneurship from a different perspective. This helps justify sport entrepreneurship as a recognized and important area to study in its own right. Sport entrepreneurship theory can aid understanding of the entrepreneurial skills needed in sport. A wider range of sport entrepreneurship studies is required to expand current research.

In this book, I seek to steer the conversation towards utilizing sport entrepreneurship in more future work. I hope this book in providing an overview of sport entrepreneurship will motivate more usage from researchers, policy planners and managers. In understanding how to create a culture supportive of entrepreneurship in sport, one of the most useful approaches is through examples. This helps people understand the process by investigating the advantages and disadvantages of sport entrepreneurship.

This book builds on prior efforts to link the fields of entrepreneurship and sport management. Sport entrepreneurship is intended to create value in a sports context by being innovative. More research is required on sport entrepreneurship in order to broaden and enrich current dialogue about the subject. Although there is still a lack of understanding about the way sport entrepreneurship fits into the mainstream entrepreneurship field, this book provides a unifying theoretical framework for future research. This book emphasizes that sport entrepreneurship will be an influential field in the future. The initial motivation behind this book was to examine entrepreneurship in sport by offering an overview of this fertile and unique area of study. This is due to sport undergoing changes resulting from internationalization and have experienced more commercialization. I hope this book stimulates the reader's curiosity in sport entrepreneurship. The transition of many sport organizations to be more entrepreneurial allows for the study of business creation.

It is anticipated that this book will make a valuable contribution to the sport management and entrepreneurship literature. The results of this book prove that sport entrepreneurship is important for economic survival but also for the solid cohesion of society. This important part of the global economy needs to be acknowledged and support given to understanding its potential. Thus, this book helps to increase awareness about the role of entrepreneurship in sport. It is important for all levels of society from consumers to business managers to incorporate entrepreneurial thinking when analyzing sport policy. In this book I make an important theoretical contribution of broadening the scope of existing research on sport entrepreneurship by identifying new paths. Thus, this book can enrich the sport management literature by showing that entrepreneurship is needed.

This book provides important managerial implications for organizations to utilize the potential of sport entrepreneurship. It is important that managers incorporate entrepreneurship in new products and services. This may require coordination between managers, innovators and other stakeholders in the process of entrepreneurship. Now the time is right for more scholars to focus on sport entrepreneurship due to the opportunities of inter-disciplinary research. The reason for this came from my interest in sport entrepreneurship stemming from the observation that despite the dominance of sport in many aspects of life including the business world and community sector there was a failure to focus on this topic in academic literature. Given the increased emphasis on entrepreneurship and innovation in society, the goal of this book was to highlight the development of a new research stream within business management studies. I endeavoured in this book to provide an overview of sports entrepreneurship and to set the stage for future research. This is due to there being an acceleration in interest on sport entrepreneurship due partly to the increased focus on sport in business and society. This book advances the field of sport entrepreneurship by supplementing the existing research by extending it to the more mainstream entrepreneurship and innovation fields. Sport entrepreneurship research has the capability of being a key field within the broader context of entrepreneurship studies.

10.4   Future Research Paths

There are interesting research paths emerging from sport entrepreneurship made more complicated by the international dimensions. Sport organizations perform a range of entrepreneurship functions including being innovative and creative that often depend on the international context. Moreover, there are cultural and social roles sport plays that are different depending on whether a country is emerging, developing or developed in economic status. Sport organizations are one of the key drivers for entrepreneurship and internationalization. Thus, there is a need for research on the genesis of entrepreneurship in sport in order to distinguish it from other environmental settings. Sport provides a specific context for studying entrepreneurship that needs to be researched and sport entrepreneurship uses synchronization of market appeal in order to develop new products and services. To enter the market successfully these innovations need to be orchestrated in terms of market entry and required resources.

Future researchers of sport entrepreneurship need to focus on how to create accurate studies about the innovation processes in sport. This will make a difference to uncovering new understandings about sport entrepreneurship. Most of the future research around sport entrepreneurship will advance the study of this discipline by including more descriptive analysis techniques. I believe that the challenge of future researchers on sport entrepreneurship will be to include more longitudinal studies about the changing business dynamics. This will benefit the field of sport research and enable the embarking of new research paths. The sports entrepreneurship field has only lately become popular. Recently research interest in sport entrepreneurship has moved rapidly in terms of publications and interest in the media. Therefore, this book will assess the sport entrepreneurship field in terms of past, present and future research. This will help establish sports entrepreneurship as a key area of business management and generate deeper academic roots in order to facilitate further interest. Table 10.1 suggests the reasons for studying sport entrepreneurship and some potential questions to ask that will help future researchers.

A challenge for future research about sport entrepreneurship is to encompass theoretical frameworks from other fields to enrich the existing research. This will enable better conceptual underpinnings to emerge that inform both theory and practice about sports entrepreneurship. There are plenty of research opportunities for sport entrepreneurship due to the range of different types of entrepreneurship. Some future research may find it difficult to focus on a specific area of sport entrepreneurship such as social due to its impact on other areas. Thus, there will be divergent paths that sport entrepreneurship will take that need to be focused into a specific area if there is to be an in-depth understanding. For example, the social part of sports entrepreneurship needs to be further legitimized as a way of understanding non-profit and volunteer components of sport business.

The inquiry about social entrepreneurship in sport needs to continue as it is an interesting area to study. Moreover, sports organizations are demanding more entrepreneurship so researchers will find helpful links with industry. This makes sport entrepreneurship worthy of research attention. I strongly believe sport entrepreneurship will develop in the same fast fashion like social, and other forms of

Table 10.1 Research questions for sports entrepreneurship

Reasons	Questions to ask
How to study sport entrepreneurship?	What methods are most appropriate? What kind of novel approaches are needed to understand sports entrepreneurship?
What to study when studying sport entrepreneurship?	What is the definition of sports entrepreneurship? What is the impact of studying sport entrepreneurship?
When do we study sport entrepreneurship?	At what stages of the sport entrepreneurship process do we conduct studies? How are studies on sport entrepreneurship designed?
Where to study sport entrepreneurship?	What profit, non-profit and hybrid forms of sport organizations should be studied?What are the most relevant environmental contexts to study sport entrepreneurship?
Who to study about sport entrepreneurship?	Who are the entities to study? Who are the stakeholders involved in sport entrepreneurship?

Adapted from Bengtsson et al. (2010), Ratten (2010, 2011)

entrepreneurship have done in the past. Hence, I advocate a number of research paths about sport entrepreneurship going forward. By researching different areas of sport and its link to entrepreneurship I expect a big increase in scholarship in this area. New knowledge about sport entrepreneurship will further cement the importance of this field. I suggest there are a number of directions sport entrepreneurship can take such as:

1. What new theories can be developed about sport entrepreneurship that take an interdisciplinary perspective?

    At the moment there are limited theories utilized to understand sport entrepreneurship as it is a new research area. Sport-based entrepreneurship theory is the theoretical framework of most research about sport and entrepreneurship but there could be new theories developed that add to current body of literature. This includes focusing on theories that can explain how entrepreneurship is different in sport due to the combination of profit-and non-profit initiatives.

2. Does other entrepreneurship literature offer models that can be used to develop the field of sport entrepreneurship?

    Currently most of the research about sport entrepreneurship focuses on business or social ventures but there is a need to study other areas of entrepreneurship. This includes more research about technology innovation occurring in sport and the role of mobile commerce in impacting the development of sport businesses. In addition, there may be cultural contexts that impact the development of sport entrepreneurship, which need to be integrated into conceptual models and theoretical frameworks that can be researched in more detail.

3. What are the key components of sport entrepreneurship?

    Sport-based entrepreneurship theory suggests that there are numerous different types of innovative activity such as economic, environmental, international, institutional, social and technological that are evident in sport. However, there are different units of analysis in terms of individual, team and society that have different conceptualizations about the role of entrepreneurship in sport. This means that the components of sport entrepreneurship in terms of the ingredients needed for a successful venture need to be understood. For example, the experience or networks of an individual might be more important than funding availability. Moreover, fans or ancillary individuals involved in sport such as psychologists might enable different types of entrepreneurship to be developed.

4. How does the sport environment contribute to entrepreneurial behavior in terms of leadership and new venture creation?

   Coaches and management play an important part of the development of entrepreneurship in sport. This is due to cross-sector collaboration being an important way to gain access to knowledge and innovation (Ratten et al. 2018). Thus, it is important to research how new venture creation is based on individual visions or team-based collaboration in sport. New venture creation can occur as part of the need for performance improvements in sport that are necessitated by the competitive nature of the industry. There are also new forms of play in sport that are a result of better data analytics that need to understood in more detail. This is due to sport being a form of entertainment so the role of entrepreneurship in this process needs to be explored.

5. What environmental context enhances the entrepreneurial capabilities of sport organizations?

   There are amateur, community and professional types of sport organizations that are all involved in different ways in the process of entrepreneurship (Miragaia et al. 2017). However, due to the increase in public-private partnerships there needs to be consideration of how the environment affects sport entrepreneurship. This is due to the need of the government to focus on certain policies and fund sport ventures around these themes (Ratten and Ferreira 2017). Alternatively, the international environment with more easier communication affects the development of innovations. This is evident in sport communities that are online enabling the discussion and dissemination about new product and service ideas.

10.5   Conclusion

This book highlights a number of ongoing discussions around the role of entrepreneurship in sport including how to plan and build entrepreneurial products, processes and services. I believe that more research is required about the role of sport entrepreneurship in society to shed light on how it can be better utilized. This book has provided guidelines and suggestions about how to develop the research stream of 'sport entrepreneurship'. In summary, the goal of this book is to improve our understanding of sport entrepreneurship. The chapters in this book build on each other by discussing different types of entrepreneurship occurring in sport. I hope that you enjoy reading this book and that its content provides a way to increase the conversation about sport entrepreneurship.

References

Bengtsson, M., Kock, S., Lundgren-Henriksson, E. L., & Nasholm, M. (2010). Coopetition research in theory and practice: Growing new theoretical, empirical and methodological domains. *Industrial Marketing Management, 57*, 4–11.

Miragaia, D. A., Ferreira, J., & Ratten, V. (2017). Corporate social responsibility and social entrepreneurship: Drivers of sports sponsorship policy. *International Journal of Sport Policy and Politics*, 1–11.

Palalic, R., Ramadani, V., Dizdarevic, A., Dilovic, A., & Ratten, V. (2017). Entrepreneurial intentions of university students: A case-based study. *Journal of Enterprising Communities: People and Places in the Global Economy, 11*(3), 393–413.

Ramadani, V., Dana, L. P., Ratten, V., & Tahiri, S. (2015). The context of Islamic entrepreneurship and business: Concept, principles and perspectives.*International. Journal of Business and Globalisation, 15*(3), 244–261.

Ratten, V. (2010). The future of sports management: A social responsibility, philanthropy and entrepreneurship perspective. *Journal of Management & Organization, 16*(04), 488–494.

Ratten, V. (2011). Social entrepreneurship and innovation in sports. *International Journal of Social Entrepreneurship and Innovation, 1*(1), 42–54.

Ratten, V., & Dana, L.-P. (2017). Gendered perspective of indigenous entrepreneurship. *Small Enterprise Research, 24*(1), 62–72.

Ratten, V., & Ferreira, J. J. (2017). Entrepreneurship, innovation and sport policy: Implications for future research. *International Journal of Sport Policy and Politics, 9*(4), 575–577.

Ratten, V., Ferreira, J. J., & Fernandes, C. I. (2017). Innovation management – Current trends and future directions. *International Journal of Innovation and Learning, 22*(2), 135–155.

Ratten, V., Marques, C. S., & Braga, V. (2018). Knowledge, learning and innovation: Research into cross-sector collaboration. In *Knowledge, learning and innovation* (pp. 1–4). London: Springer.

Made in the USA
Monee, IL
22 November 2019